SUSHI

mc rae PUBLISHING

This book was conceived, edited and designed by
McRae Publishing Ltd, London

Food Flix series
Project Director: Anne McRae   Art Director: Marco Nardi

SUSHI: DOP and Camera Operator Brent Parker Jones   Camera Operator and
Editor Adam Dyson   Hands and Food Prep Chef Ikuei Arakane   Food Stylist
Lee Blaylock   Assistant Rochelle Seator   Text Ikuei Arakane, Carla Bardi   Text
Editing Wendy Smith

ISBN 978-1-910122-27-3

Printed in Italy

FoodFlix

IKUEI ARAKANE
CARLA BARDI
SUSHI

25 VIDEO RECIPES

mc
rae
PUBLISHING

Contents

Introduction 11

How This Book Works 12

Sushi Rice 14

Small Sushi Rolls 18

Small Inside-Out Sushi Rolls 22

Large Sushi Rolls 26

Non-Traditional Large Sushi Rolls 32

Large Inside-Out Sushi Rolls 36

Bo Sushi 42

Sushi Cones 46

Pressed Sushi 50

Nigiri 56

Omelet Nigiri 60

Warship Sushi 64

Sushi Balls 68

Stuffed Squid Sushi 72

Scattered Sushi, Edo Style 76

Scattered Sushi, Kansi Style 80

Tofu Pouch Sushi 84

Moneybag Sushi 88

Children's Sushi 92

Sashimi 96

Sashimi Salads 100

Miso Soups 104

Salads 108

Garnishes 112

Pickles & Sauces 116

Index 120

Introduction

EVERYONE LOVES SUSHI! And for good reason. Sushi is healthy, fresh, and light and also great fun to serve and eat. Based on a simple mixture of vinegared rice and a huge selection of superfresh fillings, sushi can be rolled, tossed, tucked, and pressed into an endless array of exquisite dishes. In this book we will show you how to prepare all the main sushi types, from simple rolls and cones to more elaborate dishes, such as nigiri and tofu pouch sushi. We have also included recipes for miso soups, salads, sashimi, and garnishes, so that you can serve complete Japanese-style meals.

HOW THIS BOOK WORKS

This book offers a completely new approach to cooking. Our aim is to teach you the basic techniques of sushi-making by watching the videos or following the step-by-step photography so that you learn, for example, how to make perfect sushi rolls. We also give you a few variations on the basic techniques for practise, by which time we think you will be confident enough to prepare other classic dishes you may know from visits to sushi restaurants, or to invent your own variations.

Each mini-chapter presents one main recipe, plus variations.

To launch the videos, aim the eye of your device at the pictures marked by a white arrow on a red dot.

The main picture presents the final result of the main recipe.

MAKES **4 ROLLS (24 PIECES)** PREPARATION **45 MINUTES** • TIME FOR THE RICE

Small Inside-out Sushi Rolls

THESE slender, inside-out rolls are known in Japanese as *ura hosomaki.*

AVOCADO INSIDE-OUT ROLLS

Vinegar Water
1   cup (250 ml) cold water
1-2 tablespoons rice vinegar

Rolls
1   avocados
2   nori sheets
½   recipe sushi rice
     (see pages 14–17)
     Wasabi paste (optional)
2   tablespoons black sesame seeds
     Pickled ginger and fresh
     cucumber, to garnish

LIKE the very popular California sushi rolls and other large inside out rolls, ura hosomaki are not traditionally Japanese, although nowadays they are also served in Japan. These narrow rolls normally have just one main filling ingredient. We have suggested three different fillings, but once you have mastered the technique, follow your tastes to create a host of different fillings. Ura hosomaki are very attractive, delicately delicious, and they make a great appetizer and an eye-catching addition to a buffet or party spread.

OPPOSITE: AVOCADO INSIDE-OUT ROLLS

The numbered steps of the preparation are accurately described.

If you are new to sushi-making, we think the video will be very helpful. But we have also included detailed step-by-step photography, drawn from the videos, showing each main recipe as a sequence of numbered photograms with explanatory texts. The level of detail will ensure that you learn to make perfect sushi!

Inside-out Rolls with Avocado
Step by step

1. Vinegar Water: Mix the water and vinegar in a small bowl. Set aside.
2. Cover a bamboo sushi mat with plastic wrap (cling film).
3. Cut the nori sheets in half across the grain using a sharp knife or kitchen scissors.
4. Use a sharp knife to cut the avocado in half around the pit. Twist and pull the halves apart. Remove the pit. Cut into quarters and then into ½-inch (1-cm) thick slices. Remove the peel.
5. Place a sheet of nori on the bottom half of the sushi mat. The grain of the nori should be horizontally across the mat.
6. Dip your fingers in the vinegar water. Take up a handful of rice and squeeze gently into an even log.
7. Place in the center of the nori sheet and spread out evenly. Leave a ½ inch (1 cm) rice-free border along the top edge.
8. Sprinkle ½ tablespoon of sesame seeds evenly over the rice.
9. Pick up the rice-covered nori sheet and flip it over on the mat.
10. Dab some wasabi on your fingertip and spread across the center of the nori. Cover with the avocado.
11. Lift the closest edge of the mat and roll it over the filling until the two edges of nori meet. You should be able to see the rice-free border. Lift the edge of the mat a little and keep rolling. The moisture in the rice will stick the two pieces of nori together, sealing the roll.
12. Place two rolls next to each other on a clean dry chopping board. Dip a sharp knife in the vinegar water. Slice the rolls in half.
13. Slice each half roll into three even pieces. Repeat with the other rolls.
14. If liked, leave longer pieces of roll to make the finished dish more attractive.
15. Arrange on serving plates, garnish with ginger and cucumber, and serve.

VARIATION MAKES **4 ROLLS (24 PIECES)** PREPARATION **30 MINUTES** • TIME FOR THE RICE

Inside-out Rolls with Smoked Salmon & Dill

Vinegar Water
1   cup (250 ml) cold water
1-2 tablespoons rice vinegar

Rolls
½   nori sheets
½   recipe sushi rice (see pages 14–17)
2   tablespoons white sesame seeds
     Wasabi paste
5   ounces (150 g) thinly sliced smoked salmon
     Fresh dill, thinly sliced lemon, and pickled ginger, to garnish

· Prepare the vinegar water.
· Cover a bamboo sushi mat with plastic wrap (cling film).
· Cut the nori sheets in half
· Place a nori sheet on the bottom half of the bamboo mat.
· Dip your hands in the vinegar water and spread the nori evenly with the rice.

· Sprinkle with sesame seeds.
· Pick up the rice-covered sheet of nori and flip it over on the mat.
· Dab wasabi across the center of the nori. Cover with a slice of salmon and some dill.
· Roll up following the instructions in the video or step by step. Repeat with the remaining ingredients.
· Slice the rolls. Arrange on serving dishes, garnish, and serve.

VARIATION MAKES **4 ROLLS (24 PIECES)** PREPARATION **30 MINUTES** • TIME FOR THE RICE · COOKING **1 MINUTE**

Inside-out Rolls with Scallops & Cilantro

Vinegar Water
1   cup (250 ml) cold water
1-2 tablespoons rice vinegar

Rolls
1-2 tablespoons vegetable oil
5   ounces (150 g) fresh scallops, orange coral discarded, sliced
2   sheets of nori
½   recipe sushi rice (see pages 14–17)
     Watercress and carrot curls, to garnish

· Prepare the vinegar water.
· Heat the oil in a small frying pan over medium heat. Add the scallops and sear for 30 seconds on each side. Set aside.
· Cover a bamboo sushi mat with plastic wrap (cling film).
· Cut the nori sheets in half.
· Dip your hands in the vinegar water and spread the nori evenly with the rice.

· Pick up the rice-covered sheet of nori and flip it over on the mat.
· Spread a row of scallops down the center. Cover with cilantro.
· Roll up following the instructions in the video or step by step. Repeat with the remaining ingredients.
· Slice the rolls. Arrange on serving dishes, garnish, and serve.

URA HOSOMAKI 25

Variations on the main recipe share the same general preparation. The video and step-by-step sequences teach the basic technique, the variations allow you to create new dishes.

For your convenience, each recipe includes a serves line at the top with information on how many people it serves, and how long it takes to prepare and cook.

Three easy steps:

1

DOWNLOAD the free **FoodFlix App** from the Apple Store or Google Play onto your device (smartphone or tablet).

**FOODFLIX APP
IS FOR IOS
AND ANDROID**

The **FoodFlix App** can be downloaded for free, it's light on your device's memory, and is available for iOS (from the Apple

Store) or Android (from Google Play) smartphones and tablets.

The FoodFlix app icon as shown on Google Play and Apple Store

2

LAUNCH the app and scan the pictures marked with a white arrow on a red dot.

The videos all last between 1–3 minutes. The length of each video is shown on the bottom right hand of the images marked with the arrow and dot.

1:53

3

ENJOY the video (with or without background music).

NO INTERNET? NO PROBLEM!
Your internet connection is not working? Your kitchen is in a blind spot wifi-wise? Don't worry, you can still use the app. In fact, once you have downloaded it onto your device, the **FoodFlix App** doesn't need the internet at all. And if you inadvertently delete the app from your device, just go back to the Apple Store or Google Play and download it again.

REMEMBER ...

NO BOOK, NO VIDEOS

Because the videos are activated by flashing the photographs in the book marked by the white arrow on the red dot, the **FoodFlix App** can only be used if you have the book. No book, no videos!

Sushi Rice

SUSHI is a generic term for food served with cooked, vinegared rice. In Japanese, rice prepared in this way is called *sushi-meshi*.

1:26

SUSHI RICE

2	cups (400 g) sushi rice (short-grain sticky rice)
2	cups (500 ml) water
1	(2 x 3-inch/5 x 7.5-cm) piece kombu (optional)
3	tablespoons sugar
½	cup (120 ml) Japanese rice vinegar
1½	teaspoons salt

SUSHI is made using short-grain white rice that is boiled then carefully mixed with a slightly sweet vinegar mixture. Although sticky, well prepared sushi-meshi is harder and chewier than plain boiled rice because slightly less water is used to cook it. Quick cooling of the rice while constantly tossing is key to success. The tossing is traditionally done in a shallow wooden tub made of Japanese cyprus, called a hangiri. These are expensive and can be difficult to find outside of Japan but you can use any wide, shallow vessel just as long as it is not metal (which may react with the vinegar to create an unpleasant taste).

OPPOSITE: SUSHI RICE

Sushi Rice
Step by step

1. Put the rice in a large bowl and cover with cold running water.

2. Stir the rice with your hand to remove the starch. This will take 3–4 minutes.

3. Pour the rice into a colander and set aside to rest for 30–60 minutes.

4. Pour the rice into a medium saucepan and add the water.

5. If using kombu (which will add extra flavor), use kitchen scissors to make a few cuts into it to release flavor during cooking.

6. Place the pan with the rice and water over medium-high heat, cover with the lid, and bring to a boil. Reduce the heat to low and simmer for 15 minutes. Turn off the heat and let stand, still covered, for 15 minutes.

7. Combine the sugar, rice vinegar, and salt in a small saucepan.

8. Gently heat the pan, stirring occasionally, until the sugar has dissolved.

9. Remove from the heat. Pour into a glass pitcher (jug) and set aside to cool a little.

10. Remove and discard the kombu from the rice.

11. Transfer the rice to a hangiri or large shallow bowl.

12. Pour the vinegar mixture into the rice over a rice paddle or flat wooden spoon.

13. Gently toss the rice with the wooden paddle or spoon using horizontal, cutting strokes, taking care not to damage the grains of rice. Continue to gently toss until the rice is cooled, sticky, and with a glossy sheen. This will take about 10 minutes.

14. Use a fan or rolled up newspaper to cool the rice as you work.

15. If not using the rice at once, cover it with a clean damp cloth and move to a cool place. Do not refrigerate and always serve on the same day as making.

VARIATION SERVES **4–6** PREPARATION **30 MINUTES** + **30–60 MINUTES TO REST** COOKING **40 MINUTES**

Brown Sushi Rice

Although brown rice is not traditional, you can use it to make sushi. It can add flavor and texture to many dishes. Because brown rice is not as sticky, it works best in sushi where the seaweed is on the outside to keep things together. Plain, small or large rolls and cones work best, as well as scattered sushi dishes. Just remember that brown rice has more flavor than white rice and will overpower very delicate ingredients.

The method for making brown sushi rice is slightly simpler than for white rice, but the rice does take longer to cook.

2	cups (400 g) short-grain brown rice
6	cups (1.5 liters) water
½	cup (120 ml) Japanese rice vinegar
3	tablespoons honey (or sugar)
1½	teaspoons salt

• Wash the rice in a plenty of cold running water for a few seconds. Brown rice doesn't need to be rinsed as thoroughly or for as long as white rice.

• Pour the rice into a colander and set aside to stand for 30–60 minutes.

• Combine the rice and water in a medium saucepan. Place the pan over medium-high heat, cover with the lid, and bring to a boil. Reduce the heat to low and simmer for 40 minutes. Remove from the heat.

• While the rice is cooking, whisk the rice vinegar, honey, and salt in a bowl until well mixed.

• Transfer the hot rice to a hangiri or large shallow bowl. Drizzle with the vinegar mixture while tossing gently with a wooden rice paddle or flat spoon. Take care not to damage the grains of rice. Continue to gently toss the rice using horizontal, cutting strokes, until cooled, sticky, and with a glossy sheen. This will take about 10 minutes.

• Use a fan or rolled up newspaper to help cool the rice.

• If not using the rice at once, cover it with a clean damp cloth and set aside in a cool place.

• Prepared sushi rice will keep well at cool room temperature for up to about six hours, so always use the same day, and do not refrigerate as this will dry out the rice and make it difficult to press into fingers, balls, etc.

MAKES **4 ROLLS (24 PIECES)** PREPARATION **30 MINUTES + TIME FOR THE RICE**

Small Sushi Rolls

THESE small, thin rolls are known as *hosomaki*.

"*Hoso*" means small or slender in Japanese.

TUNA & WASABI ROLLS

Vinegar Water

1	cup (250 ml) cold water
1–2	tablespoons rice vinegar

Rolls

6	ounces (180 g) sashimi-quality fresh tuna steak, sliced ½ inch (1 cm) thick
2	nori sheets
	Wasabi paste
½	recipe sushi rice (see pages 14–17)
	Banana leaf, pickled ginger, thinly sliced lemon, and fresh dill, to garnish

HOSOMAKI are thin cylindrical rolls usually filled with rice and just one or two ingredients, such as tuna, cucumber, or avocado. The nori is wrapped around the outside. These rolls are usually only about 1 inch (2.5 cm) in diameter. If liked, prepare a varied platter with two or three different fillings. You can make these simple rolls more attractive by adding a brightly colored topping, such as the salmon caviar in the recipe on page 21.

OPPOSITE: TUNA & WASABI ROLLS

Tuna & Wasabi Rolls
Step by step

1. Vinegar Water: Mix the water and vinegar in a small bowl. Set aside.
2. Rolls: Cover a bamboo sushi mat with plastic wrap (cling film).
3. Cut the nori sheets in half across the grain using a sharp knife or kitchen scissors.
4. Slice the tuna into strips about the width of a pencil. Try to get four 8-inch (20-cm) strips, but you may get shorter pieces which is OK as you can put more than one into each roll.
5. Place a sheet of nori shiny side down on the bottom half of the mat. The grain of the nori should lie horizontally across the mat.
6. Dip your fingers in the vinegar water. Take up a handful of rice and squeeze it gently into an even log.
7. Place the rice in the center of the nori and spread evenly with your fingertips. Leave a ½-inch (1-cm) rice-free border along the top edge of the nori. Tidy up the left and right edges with your fingertips.
8. Put some wasabi on your finger and dab it down the center of the rice.

VARIATION   MAKES **4 ROLLS (24 PIECES)**   PREPARATION **30 MINUTES + TIME FOR THE RICE**

Cucumber Rolls

Vinegar Water
1   cup (250 ml) cold water
1–2   tablespoons rice vinegar
Rolls
2   nori sheets
1   small thin cucumber, with peel
½   recipe sushi rice (see pages 14–17)
   Wasabi paste

• Prepare the vinegar water.

• Cover a bamboo sushi mat with plastic wrap (cling film).

• Cut the nori sheets in half.

• Cut the ends off the cucumber.

Cut in half lengthwise, then into quarters. Cut out the seeds.

• Place a nori sheet on the bottom half of the bamboo mat.

• Dip your hands in the vinegar water and spread the nori evenly with the rice.

• Dab wasabi paste to taste down the center of the rice. Cover with a stick of cucumber.

• Roll up following the instructions in the video or step by step. Repeat with the remaining ingredients.

• Slice the rolls.

• Arrange on one or more serving dishes, and serve.

Place a strip of tuna on the wasabi. If you have more then one strip, arrange them end-to-end down the center of the rice.

9. Holding the filling in place with your fingers, lift the closest edge of the mat and roll it over the filling. Remove your fingers and roll until the two edges of nori meet. You should be able to see the rice-free border. Lift the edge of the mat and keep rolling.

The moisture in the rice will stick the two pieces of nori together, sealing the roll. Carefully remove the mat and set the roll aside while you make the other rolls.

10. Place two rolls next to each other on a clean dry chopping board. Dip a sharp knife into the vinegar water. Slice the rolls in half, and then slice each half roll into three even pieces.

11. If liked, slice some pieces of the rolls diagonally, to make the finished dish more attractive.

12. Arrange the rolls on one or more serving plates. If liked, place a banana leaf on each plate and cover with the rolls. Garnish with the pickled ginger, lemon, and dill, and serve.

VARIATION MAKES **4 ROLLS (24 PIECES)** PREPARATION **30 MINUTES + TIME FOR THE RICE**

Fresh Salmon & Avocado Rolls with Salmon Roe

Vinegar Water
1   cup (250 ml) cold water
1–2 tablespoons rice vinegar

Rolls
2   nori sheets
1   avocado, peeled, pitted, and cut into long thin strips
3   ounces (90 g) sashimi-quality salmon steak, skin and bones removed
½   recipe sushi rice (see pages 14–17)
    Wasabi paste
2   ounces (60 g) salmon roe

• Prepare the vinegar water.

• Cover a bamboo sushi mat with plastic wrap (cling film).

• Cut the nori sheets in half.

• Cut the salmon into long strips about ½ inch (1 cm) wide.

• Place a nori sheet on the bottom half of the bamboo mat.

• Dip your hands in the vinegar water and spread the nori evenly with the rice.

• Dab wasabi paste down the center of the rice. Cover with a line of salmon and avocado.

• Roll up following the instructions in the video or step by step. Repeat with the remaining ingredients.

• Slice the rolls. Spoon salmon roe onto the tops.

• Arrange on serving dishes, and serve.

Small Inside-Out Sushi Rolls

THESE slender, inside-out rolls are known in Japanese as *ura hosomaki*.

1:53

LIKE the very popular California sushi rolls and other large inside-out rolls, ura hosomaki are not traditionally Japanese, although nowadays they are also served in Japan. These narrow rolls normally have just one main filling ingredient. We have suggested three different fillings, but once you have mastered the technique, follow your tastes to create a host of different fillings. Ura hosomaki are very attractive, delicately delicious, and they make a great appetizer and an eye-catching addition to a buffet or party spread.

AVOCADO INSIDE-OUT ROLLS

Vinegar Water

1	cup (250 ml) cold water
1–2	tablespoons rice vinegar

Rolls

1	avocado
2	nori sheets
½	recipe sushi rice (see pages 14–17)
	Wasabi paste (optional)
2	tablespoons black sesame seeds
	Pickled ginger and fresh cucumber, to garnish

OPPOSITE: AVOCADO INSIDE-OUT ROLLS

Inside-out Rolls with Avocado
Step by step

1. Vinegar Water: Mix the water and vinegar in a small bowl. Set aside.

2. Rolls: Cover a bamboo sushi mat with plastic wrap (cling film).

3. Cut the nori sheets in half across the grain using a sharp knife or kitchen scissors.

4. Use a sharp knife to cut the avocado in half around the pit. Twist and pull the halves apart. Remove the pit. Cut into quarters and then into ½-inch (1-cm) thick slices. Remove the peel.

5. Place a sheet of nori on the bottom half of the sushi mat. The grain of the nori should lie horizontally across the mat.

6. Dip your fingers in the vinegar water. Take up a handful of rice and squeeze gently into an even log.

7. Place in the center of the nori sheet and spread out evenly. Leave a ½-inch (1-cm) rice-free border along the top edge.

8. Sprinkle ½ tablespoon of sesame seeds evenly over the rice.

9. Pick up the rice-covered nori sheet and flip it over on the mat.

10. Dab some wasabi on your fingertip and spread across the center of the nori. Cover with the avocado.

11. Lift the closest edge of the mat and roll it over the filling until the two edges of nori meet. You should be able to see the rice-free border. Lift the edge of the mat a little and keep rolling. The moisture in the rice will stick the two pieces of nori together, sealing the roll.

12. Place two rolls next to each other on a clean dry chopping board. Dip a sharp knife into the vinegar water. Slice the rolls in half.

13. Slice each half roll into three even pieces. Repeat with the other rolls.

14. If liked, leave longer pieces of roll to make the finished dish more attractive.

15. Arrange on serving plates, garnish with ginger and cucumber, and serve.

VARIATION MAKES **4 ROLLS (24 PIECES)** PREPARATION **30 MINUTES + TIME FOR THE RICE**

Inside-Out Rolls with Smoked Salmon & Dill

Vinegar Water
1	cup (250 ml) cold water
1–2	tablespoons rice vinegar

Rolls
2	nori sheets
½	recipe sushi rice (see pages 14–17)
2	tablespoons white sesame seeds
	Wasabi paste
5	ounces (150 g) thinly sliced smoked salmon
	Fresh dill, thinly sliced lemon, and pickled ginger, to garnish

- Prepare the vinegar water.
- Cover a bamboo sushi mat with plastic wrap (cling film).
- Cut the nori sheets in half.
- Place a nori sheet on the bottom half of the bamboo mat.
- Dip your hands in the vinegar water and spread the nori evenly with the rice.
- Sprinkle with sesame seeds.
- Pick up the rice-covered sheet of nori and flip it over on the mat.
- Dab wasabi across the center of the nori. Cover with a slice of salmon and some dill.
- Roll up following the instructions in the video or step by step. Repeat with the remaining ingredients.
- Slice the rolls. Arrange on serving dishes, garnish, and serve.

VARIATION MAKES **4 ROLLS (24 PIECES)** PREPARATION **30 MINUTES + TIME FOR THE RICE** COOKING **1 MINUTE**

Inside-Out Rolls with Scallops & Cilantro

Vinegar Water
1	cup (250 ml) cold water
1–2	tablespoons rice vinegar

Rolls
1–2	tablespoons vegetable oil
5	ounces (150 g) fresh scallops, orange coral discarded, sliced
2	nori sheets
½	recipe sushi rice (see pages 14–17)
½	cup fresh cilantro (coriander) leaves
	Watercress and carrot curls, to garnish

- Prepare the vinegar water.
- Heat the oil in a small frying pan over medium heat. Add the scallops and sear for 30 seconds on each side. Set aside.
- Cover a bamboo sushi mat with plastic wrap (cling film).
- Cut the nori sheets in half.
- Place a nori sheet on the bottom half of the bamboo mat.
- Dip your hands in the vinegar water and spread the nori evenly with the rice.
- Pick up the rice-covered sheet of nori and flip it over on the mat.
- Spread a row of scallops down the center. Cover with cilantro.
- Roll up following the instructions in the video or step by step. Repeat with the remaining ingredients.
- Slice the rolls. Arrange on serving dishes, garnish, and serve.

Large Sushi Rolls

LARGE ROLLS, or *futomaki*, as they are known in Japanese, are one of the most popular types of sushi, especially outside of Japan.

1:59

FUTOMAKI are thick or fat cylindrical rolls of filled rice, wrapped with the nori on the outside. Futomaki are usually about 2 inches (5 cm) in diameter and often contain two, three, or more fillings that are chosen for their complementary tastes and colors. Traditionally filled with some kind of fresh fish, these rolls lend themselves to many different fillings and need not contain fish at all. Brown rice works well in these rolls, especially with vegetarian fillings. Once you have learned the basic technique, you will enjoy inventing new fillings for an array of tasty rolls.

SALMON, CRAB & AVOCADO ROLLS

Vinegar Water

1	cup (250 ml) cold water
1–2	tablespoons rice vinegar

Rolls

6	ounces (180 g) sashimi-quality salmon steak, skin and bones removed
2	avocados
4	nori sheets
1	recipe sushi rice (see pages 14–17)
12	ounces (350 g) white crabmeat or imitation crabmeat sticks
	Bunch of fresh chives
	Pickles, fresh dill, and thinly sliced lemon, to garnish

OPPOSITE: SALMON, CRAB & AVOCADO ROLLS

Salmon, Crab & Avocado Rolls
Step by step

1. Vinegar Water: Mix the water and vinegar in a small bowl. Set aside.

2. Rolls: Cover a bamboo sushi mat with plastic wrap (cling film).

3. Use a sharp knife to cut the avocados in half around the pit. Twist and pull the halves apart. Remove the pit. Cut the halves into quarters, then into ½-inch (1-cm) thick slices. Peel the slices.

4. Slice the salmon into long strips about ½ inch (1 cm) wide.

5. Place a sheet of nori shiny side down on the sushi mat. The grain of the nori should lie horizontally across the mat.

6. Dip your fingers in the vinegar water. Take up two handfuls of rice and squeeze gently into an even log.

7. Place in the center of the nori sheet and spread out evenly. Leave a 1-inch (2.5-cm) rice-free border along the top edge.

8. Spread a quarter of the salmon, avocado, crabmeat, and chives across the center of the rice.

9. Holding the filling in place with your fingers, lift the closest edge of the mat and roll it over the filling. Remove your fingers and roll until the two edges of nori meet.

10. Press down on the filling gently but firmly to compact. You should be able to see the rice-free border.

11. Lift the edge of the mat a little and keep rolling. The moisture in the rice will stick the two pieces of nori together, sealing the roll.

12. Place a roll on a clean dry chopping board. Dip the blade of a sharp knife into the vinegar water and slice the roll in half.

13. Slice each half roll into four even pieces. Repeat with the remaining rolls.

14. Arrange the rolls on serving plates.

15. Garnish with pickles and lemon, and serve.

VARIATION   MAKES **4 ROLLS (32 PIECES)**   PREPARATION **30 MINUTES + TIME FOR THE RICE**

Fresh Tuna Rolls

Vinegar Water
1   cup (250 ml) cold water
1–2   tablespoons rice vinegar
Rolls
6   ounces (180 g) canned tuna, drained
1   small red onion, finely chopped
2   tablespoons finely chopped fresh parsley
2–3   tablespoons spicy mayonnaise (see page 119)
1   teaspoon karashi mustard paste
4   nori sheets
1   recipe sushi rice (see pages 14–17) Soy sauce, to serve

• Prepare the vinegar water.

• Put the tuna in a bowl and mash with a fork. Add the onion, parsley, mayonnaise, and karashi paste and mix well.

• Cover a bamboo sushi mat with plastic wrap (cling film). Place a sheet of nori shiny side down on the sushi mat.

• Dip your hands in the vinegar water and spread the nori evenly with the rice.

• Dab with wasabi and spread a quarter of the tuna salad across the center.

• Roll up following the instructions in the video or step by step. Repeat with the remaining ingredients.

• Slice the rolls, arrange on serving plates, and serve with the soy sauce.

VARIATION   MAKES **4 ROLLS (32 PIECES)**   PREPARATION **45 MINUTES**   COOKING **30–40 MINUTES**

Roasted Vegetable Rolls

Vinegar Water
1   cup (250 ml) cold water
1–2   tablespoons rice vinegar
Rolls
1   recipe sushi rice (see pages 14–17)
1   bunch asparagus, ends trimmed
3   tablespoons extra-virgin olive oil
1   teaspoon salt
4   medium carrots, sliced lengthwise into ½-inch (1-cm) sticks
1   tablespoon maple syrup
1   white onion, thinly sliced
4   nori sheets
    Wasabi paste
    Soy sauce, to serve

• Prepare the vinegar water.

• Preheat the oven to 400°F (220°C/gas 6).

• Toss the asparagus with 1 tablespoon of oil and half the salt. Toss the carrots with the maple syrup and 1 tablespoon of oil. Toss the onion with the remaining oil and salt. Spread the vegetables out in a large roasting pan. Roast for 30–40 minutes, until tender. Set aside to cool.

• Cover a bamboo sushi mat with plastic wrap (cling film). Place a sheet of nori shiny side down on the sushi mat.

• Dip your hands in the vinegar water and spread the nori evenly with the rice.

• Dab with wasabi and arrange a quarter of the vegetables across the center.

• Roll up following the instructions in the video or step by step. Repeat with the remaining ingredients.

• Slice the rolls, arrange on serving plates, and serve with the soy sauce.

Tuna, Cucumber & Scallion Rolls

Vinegar Water
1   cup (250 ml) cold water
1–2   tablespoons rice vinegar
Rolls
8   ounces (250 g) sashimi-quality fresh
       tuna
4   nori sheets
1   recipe sushi rice (see pages 14–17)
       Wasabi paste
1   small cucumber, with peel, cut
       lengthwise into 4 long strips
4   scallions (spring onions), trimmed
       Banana leaves, to serve (optional)
       Soy sauce, to serve

• Prepare the vinegar water.

• Slice the tuna into long strips about ½-inch (1-cm) wide.

• Cover a bamboo sushi mat with plastic wrap (cling film). Place a sheet of nori shiny side down on the sushi mat.

• Dip your fingers in the vinegar water. Take up the rice and spread on the nori.

• Dab wasabi across the center of the rice. Cover with a line of tuna, some cucumber, and scallions.

• Roll up following the instructions in the video or step by step. Repeat with the remaining ingredients.

• Place a roll on a clean dry chopping board. Dip the blade of a sharp knife into the vinegar water and slice the roll in half.

• Slice each half roll into four even pieces. Repeat with the remaining rolls.

• Garnish a serving platter with banana leaves, if liked, and arrange the rolls on top.

• Serve with a small bowl of soy sauce.

OPPOSITE: TUNA, CUCUMBER & SCALLION ROLLS

Teriyaki Beef Rolls

Teriyaki Beef
¼   cup (60 ml) soy sauce
¼   cup (60 ml) mirin
2   tablespoons sugar
12   ounces (350 g) rump steak,
       about ¾ inch (2 cm) thick
1   tablespoon vegetable oil
Vinegar Water
1   cup (250 ml) cold water
1–2   tablespoons rice vinegar
Rolls
4   nori sheets
1   recipe sushi rice (see pages 14–17)
       Wasabi paste
2   carrots, grated
1   cucumber, seeded and cut into long
       thin strips
       Pickled ginger and soy sauce, to serve

• Bring the soy sauce, mirin, and sugar to a boil in a small saucepan over medium heat. Simmer for 2–3 minutes. Set aside to cool.

• Marinate the steak in the teriyaki sauce in the refrigerator for 2–12 hours.

• Heat a grill pan (griddle) over medium heat and brush with the oil.

• Grill the steak until cooked to your liking, 3–4 minutes each side for medium-rare.

• Remove from the heat. Let cool a little, then cut into thin strips.

• Prepare the vinegar water.

• Cover a bamboo sushi mat with plastic wrap (cling film).

• Place a nori sheet on the bottom half of the bamboo mat.

• Dip your hands in the vinegar water and spread the nori evenly with the rice.

• Dab some wasabi across the center of the rice.

• Spread with a quarter of the beef. Top with the carrots, cucumber, and pickled ginger.

• Roll up following the instructions in the video or step by step. Repeat with the remaining ingredients.

• Place a roll on a clean dry chopping board. Dip the blade of a sharp knife into the vinegar water and slice the roll in half.

• Slice each half roll into four even pieces. Repeat with the remaining rolls.

• Arrange on serving plates and serve with the pickled ginger and soy sauce.

Shrimp & Avocado Rolls

Vinegar Water
1   cup (250 ml) cold water
1–2   tablespoons rice vinegar

Rolls
4   nori sheets
1   recipe sushi rice (see pages 14–17)
      Wasabi paste
1   cucumber, cut lengthwise into long
      thin strips
1   avocado, peeled, pitted, and cut into
      long thin strips
16   large cooked shrimp, peeled, deveined,
      and cut in half lengthwise
      Pickled ginger, to serve

• Prepare the vinegar water.

• Cover a bamboo sushi mat with plastic wrap (cling film). Place a sheet of nori shiny side down on the sushi mat.

• Dip your hands in the vinegar water and spread the nori evenly with the rice.

• Dab some wasabi across the center of the rice.

• Place strips of cucumber, avocado, and shrimp lengthwise over the wasabi.

• Roll up following the instructions in the video or step by step. Repeat with the remaining ingredients.

• Slice the rolls and arrange on serving plates. Garnish with the pickled ginger, and serve.

Non-Traditional Large Sushi Rolls

These *futomaki* are made in the traditional way but they use unusual or non-Japanese fillings or wrapping material.

In this chapter we focus on non-traditional sushi rolls. You can change the filling or the rice, or even replace the nori wrapping with something else. Fillings can include various combinations of fresh or cooked vegetables, cheeses, herbs, or meats, including deli meats. The white rice can be replaced with brown rice or even with quinoa, spelt, or pearl barley. Instead of using traditional nori to wrap the fillings, try wrapping them in ham, prosciutto, thinly sliced zucchini (courgettes), or tortillas. The only limit is your imagination!

SEARED BEEF ROLLS

Steak

1	pound (500 g) rib-eye or other well-marbled steak
¼	cup (60 ml) soy sauce
1	tablespoon brown sugar
⅓	cup (90 ml) stout
4	cloves garlic, minced
2	scallions (spring onions), minced
1	teaspoon freshly ground black pepper
2	teaspoons sesame oil
1	tablespoon honey

Vinegar Water

1	cup (250 ml) cold water
1–2	tablespoons rice vinegar

Rolls

4	nori sheets
1	recipe sushi rice (see pages 14–17)
	Chopped scallions, fresh basil, shiso, or cilantro (coriander), baby carrots, peeled and quartered, thinly sliced garlic, chili sauce
	Watercress, tomatoes, finely grated daikon, to garnish

OPPOSITE: SEARED BEEF ROLLS

Seared Beef Rolls
Step by step

1. Steak: Wrap the steak in plastic wrap (cling film) and place in the freezer.

2. Combine the soy sauce, sugar, stout, garlic, scallions, pepper, sesame oil, and honey in a bowl. Stir until dissolved.

3. Unwrap the steak and trim off any fat with a sharp knife. Cut across the grain into ¼-inch (5-mm) slices. Cut into strips.

4. Stir the steak into the marinade and let sit for 30 minutes.

5. Preheat a large frying pan over medium-high heat. Add the beef and sear for 2–3 minutes on each side.

6. Set aside to cool.

7. Cover a bamboo sushi mat with plastic wrap (cling film).

8. Place a sheet of nori shiny side down on the sushi mat. The grain of the nori should lie horizontally across the mat.

9. Vinegar Water: Mix the water and vinegar in a small bowl. Dip your fingers in the vinegar water. Take up two handfuls of the sushi rice and squeeze gently into an even log.

10. Place on the nori sheet and spread out evenly. Leave a 1-inch (2.5-cm) rice-free border free along the top edge.

11. Squirt a line of Sriracha sauce across the center of the rice. Top with a quarter of the beef.

12. Cover with a mixture of your choice of the scallions, carrots, herbs, and garlic. Don't overload the rolls.

13. Holding the filling in place with your fingers, lift the closest edge of the mat and roll it over the filling. Remove your fingers and roll until the two edges of nori meet. You should be able to see the rice-free border.

14. Lift the edge of the mat and keep rolling. The moisture in the rice will stick the pieces of nori together, sealing the roll. Tidy up the ends of the roll with a cloth.

15. Dip the blade of a sharp knife in the vinegar water. Place a roll on a clean dry chopping board and slice it in half.

16. Slice each roll in half and then in half again to make eight even pieces.

17. Arrange the rolls on a serving plate.

18. Garnish with the tomatoes, radishes, watercress, and daikon, and serve.

Smoked Salmon Sushi Wraps

1	recipe sushi rice (see pages 14–17)
6	large corn or flour tortillas or wraps
6	large slices smoked salmon
3	ounces (90 g) cream cheese, chilled, and cut into batons about the same thickness as a pencil
1	small thin cucumber, with peeled, ends trimmed, cut lengthwise into strips
6	scallions (spring onions), trimmed
2	cups (500 g) spicy tomato salsa, for dipping (optional)

• Prepare the sushi rice.

• Wrap the tortillas in slightly damp double layers of paper towels and microwave on high for 45 seconds. Alternatively, soften them one by one in an ungreased frying pan over medium heat.

• Spread some rice on each warm tortilla. Cover with a slice of salmon, and arrange a row of cream cheese, some cucumber, and a scallion down the center.

• Roll up sushi-style and use a sharp knife to slice into rolls.

• Arrange on a serving platter with the salsa for dipping, if liked, and serve.

Large Inside-Out Sushi Rolls

THESE rolls originated in California in the 1960s and have now become popular all over the world.

CALIFORNIA SUSHI ROLLS

Vinegar Water

1	cup (250 ml) cold water
1–2	tablespoons rice vinegar

Rolls

1	avocado
1	medium yellow bell pepper (capsicum)
4	nori sheets
1	recipe sushi rice (see pages 14–17)
2	tablespoons black sesame seeds
2	tablespoons mayonnaise
6	ounces (180 g) imitation crab sticks

Inside-out rolls were invented in Los Angeles in the 1960s when Japanese sushi chefs discovered that their Americans clients preferred not to see the chewy nori on the outside of the rolls. These same chefs also began replacing the traditional raw tuna in the filling with avocado, and the California roll was born. Inside-out rolls are the perfect example of "fusion" food and led chefs to experiment with many different fillings and wraps. These attractive rolls are made by flipping the nori after it has been spread with the sticky sushi rice and laying the filling directly on the nori.

OPPOSITE: CALIFORNIA SUSHI ROLLS

California Sushi Rolls
Step by step

1. Vinegar Water: Mix the water and vinegar in a small bowl and set aside.

2. Rolls: Cover a bamboo sushi mat with plastic wrap (cling film).

3. Use a sharp knife to cut the avocado in half around the pit. Twist and pull the halves apart. Remove the pit and peel the halves. Cut into ½-inch (1-cm) thick slices.

4. Cut the bell pepper in half. Scrape out the seeds, and slice lengthwise into ½-inch (1-cm) thick slices.

5. Place a sheet of nori on the sushi mat. In this case it doesn't have to be shiny side down as the nori will not be visible in the finished rolls. The grain of the nori should lie horizontally across the mat.

6. Dip your fingers into the vinegar water. Take up two handfuls of the sushi rice and squeeze them gently into an even log. Place in the center of the nori and spread out evenly with your fingertips. Leave a 1-inch (2.5-cm) rice-free border along the top edge of the sheet of nori.

VARIATION   MAKES **4 ROLLS (32 PIECES)**   PREPARATION **30 MINUTES + TIME FOR THE RICE**

Inside-Out Vegetarian Rolls

Vinegar Water
1   cup (250 ml) cold water
1–2   tablespoons rice vinegar

Rolls
4   nori sheets
1   recipe sushi rice (see pages 14–17)
2   tablespoons black sesame seeds, toasted
     Wasabi paste
1   small cucumber, with peel, trimmed and cut into thin strips lengthwise
1–2   avocados, peeled, pitted, and cut into thin strips
2   carrots, cut into thin strips lengthwise
     Pickled ginger, to serve

• Prepare the vinegar water.

• Cover a bamboo sushi mat with plastic wrap (cling film). Place a nori sheet on top.

• Dip your hands into the vinegar water and spread the nori evenly with the rice.

• Sprinkle with sesame seeds.

• Pick up the rice-covered sheet of nori and flip it over on the mat.

• Dab wasabi across the center. Cover with strips of cucumber, avocado, and carrots.

• Roll up following the instructions in the video or step by step. Repeat with the remaining ingredients.

• Slice the rolls, arrange on serving plates, and serve with the pickled ginger.

7. Sprinkle ½ tablespoon of the black sesame seeds evenly over the rice.

8. Working quickly, pick up the rice-covered sheet of nori and flip it over on the mat.

9. Spread ½ tablespoon of mayonnaise across the center of the nori. Cover with a quarter of the crab sticks, avocado, and bell pepper.

10. Holding the filling in place with your fingers, lift the closest edge of the mat and roll it over the filling. Remove your fingers and roll until the two edges of nori meet. Lift the edge of the mat a little and keep rolling. The moisture in the rice will stick the two pieces of nori together, sealing the roll. Remove the mat and set the roll aside while you make the other rolls.

11. Dip the blade of a sharp knife into the vinegar water. Place a roll on a clean dry chopping board and slice it in half. Slice each half roll in half and then in half again to make eight even pieces. Repeat with the remaining rolls.

12. Squiggle some mayonnaise on serving plates. Sprinkle with sesame seeds. Arrange the rolls decoratively on the plate, and serve.

VARIATION   MAKES **4 ROLLS (32 PIECES)**   PREPARATION **45 MINUTES + TIME FOR THE RICE**

Philadelphia Rolls

Vinegar Water
1   cup (250 ml) cold water
1–2   tablespoons rice vinegar
Rolls
4   nori sheets
1   recipe sushi rice (see pages 14–17)
8   ounces (250 g) cream cheese, chilled
1–2   avocados, peeled, pitted, and cut into thin strips
8–12 large thin slices smoked salmon

• Prepare the vinegar water.

• Cover a bamboo sushi mat with plastic wrap (cling film). Place a nori sheet on top.

• Dip your hands into the vinegar water and spread the nori evenly with the rice.

• Pick up the rice-covered sheet of nori and flip it over on the mat.

• Spread the nori evenly with a quarter of the cream cheese leaving a large border around the edges.

• Place a line of avocado across the center.

• Roll up following the instructions in the video or step by step. Repeat with the remaining ingredients.

• Wrap the rolls in the salmon, ensuring that the rice is completely covered.

• Slice the rolls, arrange on serving plates, and serve.

Inside-Out Spicy Ham & Cream Cheese Rolls

Vinegar Water
1   cup (150 ml) cold water
1–2 tablespoons rice vinegar
Rolls
4   nori sheets
1   recipe sushi rice (see pages 14–17)
2   tablespoons white sesame seeds
     Sriracha sauce, to taste
5   ounces (150 g) thinly sliced ham
1   avocado, peeled, halved, pitted, and
     sliced into ½-inch (1-cm) thick, long
     strips
1   small red or yellow bell pepper
     (capsicum) seeded, and sliced
     lengthwise into ½-inch (1-cm) thick
     strips
4   ounces (120 g) cream cheese, chilled,
     cut into batons about as thick as a
     pencil
     Pickled ginger and wasabi paste,
     to serve

• Prepare the vinegar water.

• Cover a bamboo sushi mat with plastic wrap (cling film). Place a sheet of nori on the sushi mat.

• Dip your fingers into the vinegar water. Take up the rice and spread on the nori.

• Sprinkle with sesame seeds.

• Pick up the rice-covered sheet of nori and flip it over on the mat.

• Squirt Sriracha sauce cross the center of the rice. Cover with ham, avocado, bell pepper, and cream cheese.

• Roll up following the instructions in the video or step by step. Repeat with the remaining ingredients.

• Place a roll on a clean dry chopping board. Dip the blade of a sharp knife into the vinegar water and slice the roll in half.

• Slice each half roll into four even pieces. Repeat with the remaining rolls.

• Arrange the rolls on serving plates, and serve with the wasabi paste and pickled ginger.

OPPOSITE: INSIDE-OUT SPICY HAM & CREAM CHEESE ROLLS

Inside-Out Chicken & Cream Cheese Rolls with Dill

Vinegar Water
1   cup (250 ml) cold water
1–2 tablespoons rice vinegar
Rolls
1   tablespoon vegetable oil
2   boneless skinless chicken breasts, sliced
     into thin fillets
4   nori sheets
1   recipe sushi rice (see pages 14–17)
7   ounces (200 g) cream cheese, chilled
     Wasabi paste
3–4 tablespoons coarsely chopped fresh dill

• Prepare the vinegar water.

• Heat the oil in a grill pan (griddle) over medium heat. Add the chicken and grill until cooked, 7–10 minutes. Let cool.

• Cover a bamboo sushi mat with plastic wrap (cling film). Place a nori sheet on top.

• Dip your hands into the vinegar water and spread the nori evenly with the rice.

• Pick up the rice-covered sheet of nori and flip it over on the mat.

• Spread the nori evenly with a quarter of the cream cheese. Place a line of grilled chicken across the center of the rice. Dab with wasabi.

• Roll up following the instructions in the video or step by step. Repeat with the remaining ingredients.

• Sprinkle the rolls with dill, then slice. Arrange on plates, and serve.

Inside-Out Grilled Salmon & Cream Cheese Rolls

Vinegar Water
1	cup (250 ml) cold water
1–2	tablespoons rice vinegar

Rolls
1	tablespoon vegetable oil
6	ounces (180 g) salmon fillets
4	nori sheets
1	recipe sushi rice (see pages 14–17)
7	ounces (200 g) cream cheese, chilled
1–2	cucumbers, with peel, ends trimmed and sliced very thinly lengthwise
3	ounces (90 g) salmon roe

• Prepare the vinegar water.

• Heat the oil in a grill pan (griddle) over medium heat. Add the salmon and grill until cooked, 5–8 minutes. Let cool.

• Cover a bamboo sushi mat with plastic wrap (cling film). Place a nori sheet on top.

• Dip your fingers into the vinegar water and spread the nori evenly with the rice.

• Pick up the rice-covered sheet of nori and flip it over on the mat.

• Spread the nori evenly with a quarter of the cream cheese. Place a line of grilled salmon across the center of the rice.

• Roll up following the instructions in the video or step by step. Repeat with the remaining ingredients.

• Wrap the rolls in the cucumber.

• Slice the rolls and top each one with salmon roe. Arrange on plates, and serve.

Bo Sushi

This sushi comes from the Kyoto region.

"Bo" refers to the bar shape of the pressed roll.

Bo Sushi, also known as saba sushi, comes from the inland region of Kyoto where fresh seafood was not easy to come by until recently. Bo sushi was often made using marinated mackerel or unagi (freshwater eel). Nowadays it is usually made with fresh grilled mackerel.

GRILLED MACKEREL BO SUSHI

Vinegar Water

1	cup (250 ml) cold water
1–2	tablespoons rice vinegar

Sushi

4	(5-ounce/150-g) fillets of mackerel, with skin
½	recipe sushi rice (see pages 14–17)
1	tablespoon finely chopped pickled ginger
2	finely chopped fresh shiso leaves (o cilantro/coriander)
1	tablespoon toasted black sesame seeds
	Soy sauce and wasabi paste, to serve

OPPOSITE: GRILLED MACKEREL BO SUSHI

Grilled Mackerel Bo Sushi
Step by step

Inexpensive, tasty, and packed with nutritious protein, Vitamins B12 and D, phosphorus, and omega-3 oils, mackerel is a always a healthy food choice.

1. Vinegar Water: Mix the water and vinegar in a small bowl and set aside.
2. Sushi: Lay the fillets of mackerel on a cutting board and use tweezers to remove the bones.
3. Preheat an overhead broiler (grill) in the oven on medium-high heat. Lightly grease a baking sheet.
4. Place the mackerel skin-side up under the broiler and cook for 7–8 minutes, until crisp and golden.
5. Set aside to cool.
6. Cover a bamboo sushi mat with plastic wrap (cling film).
7. Put the sushi rice in a bowl and mix in the chopped pickled ginger, shiso leaves, and sesame seeds.
8. Place two fillets of mackerel skin-side down on the prepared sushi mat.
9. Dab with some wasabi.
10. Dip your fingers into the vinegar water. Take up half the rice mixture and gently squeeze it into a log as long as the mackerel. Place it on top of the mackerel.
11. Fold the plastic wrap over the rice and fish then roll in the mat.
12. Press gently but firmly along the roll to compact it as you roll.
13. Carefully unwrap the mat but leave the plastic wrap on the roll.
14. Use a sharp knife to cut the roll in half through the plastic wrap, then cut into 5 or 6 pieces. Repeat with the remaining ingredients.
15. Arrange the bo sushi on serving plates, and serve the with soy sauce and wasabi paste.

Sushi Cones

THESE hand-rolls, or *temaki*, as they are known in Japan, are made by wrapping the nori around the rice and filling and rolling into cone shapes.

2:21

These are the easiest type of sushi to prepare. If you are entertaining friends or family casually, serve these cones as Japanese hosts often do: present your guests with sheets of nori and an array of prepared fresh ingredients laid out on a platter so that they can make up their own cones with the fillings they like best. This can be a fun way to introduce guests to homemade sushi.

MIXED SEAFOOD CONES

Vinegar Water

1	cup (250 ml) cold water
1–2	tablespoons rice vinegar

Cones

4	nori sheets
1	avocado
1	small yellow bell pepper (capsicum)
1	lemon, halved
1	small thin cucumber
1	recipe sushi rice (see pages 14–17)
	Wasabi paste
2	tablespoons black sesame seeds
5	ounces (150 g) sashimi-quality tuna fillet, cut into long thin strips
	Spicy mayonnaise (see page 119)
2	tablespoons white sesame seeds
3	ounces (90 g) smoked salmon, thinly sliced, cut into 8 pieces
8	large cooked (tiger) shrimp (prawns), shelled, heads removed, and deveined
	Finely grated daikon and shiso (perilla) leaves, to garnish

OPPOSITE: MIXED SEAFOOD CONES

Mixed Seafood Sushi Cones

Step by step

1. Use a sharp knife to cut the nori sheets in half across the grain.
2. Cut the avocado in half around the pit. Twist and pull the halves apart.

Remove the pit and peel the halves. Cut into ½-inch (1-cm) thick slices.

3. Cut the bell pepper in half. Scrape out the seeds, and slice lengthwise into ½-inch (1-cm) thick slices. Drizzle with lemon juice.
4. Cut the ends off the cucumber. Cut in half lengthwise, then into quarters. Remove the seeds. Slice lengthwise.
5. Combine the water and vinegar in a small bowl. Place a nori sheet shiny

side down on a clean cutting board. Dip your hands into the vinegar water. Spread 1–2 tablespoons of sushi rice over half of the nori sheet.

6. Dab with some wasabi and sprinkle evenly with ½ tablespoon of the black sesame seeds. Lay a quarter of the tuna, avocado, and bell pepper diagonally across the rice.
7. Roll the nori around the filling to create a cone by folding the bottom

---

VARIATION　MAKES **8 CONES**　PREPARATION **15–20 MINUTES + TIME FOR THE RICE**

Vegetarian Sushi Cones

Vinegar Water
1　cup (250 ml) cold water
1–2　tablespoons rice vinegar

Cones
4　nori sheets
1　recipe sushi rice (see pages 14–17)
　　Sriracha sauce
5　ounces (150 g) cream cheese, chilled, cut into short batons
1　cucumber, with peel, seeds removed, cut into long thin strips
2　carrots, cut into long thin strips
1　red bell pepper (capsicum), cut into long thin strips
2–3　tablespoons white sesame seeds

• Prepare the vinegar water.

• Cut the nori sheets in half.

• Place a nori sheet shiny side down on a clean cutting board. Dip your hands into the vinegar water. Spread 1–2 tablespoons of sushi rice over half of the nori sheet.

• Dab the rice with Sriracha sauce. Lay pieces of cream cheese, cucumber, carrot, and bell pepper diagonally across the rice.

• Roll up into cones following the instructions in the video or step by step. Repeat with the remaining ingredients.

• Sprinkle with the sesame seeds.

• Arrange on serving plates, and serve.

left-hand corner of the nori sheet toward the top right-hand corner and rolling to the end of the strip of nori to make a cone.

8. Stick a few grains of rice to the corner of the nori sheet and press down to seal. Repeat with three more sheets of nori and the remaining tuna, avocado, bell pepper, and black sesame seeds to make four cones.

9. Place a nori sheet shiny side down on

a clean cutting board. Dip your hands in the vinegar water. Spread 1–2 tablespoons of sushi rice over one half of the nori sheet.

10. Dab with some spicy mayonnaise and sprinkle evenly with ½ tablespoon of the white sesame seeds. Top with a piece of salmon, two shrimp, and some strips of cucumber.

11. Roll the nori around the filling to create a cone by folding the bottom

left-hand corner of the nori sheet toward the top right-hand corner and rolling to the end of the strip of nori to make a cone. Stick together with a few grains of rice. Repeat with the remaining ingredients to make four cones.

12. Garnish a serving dish or two with grated daikon and shiso leaves. Arrange the cones decoratively on the plates, and serve.

VARIATION   MAKES **8 CONES**   PREPARATION **15–20 MINUTES + TIME FOR THE RICE**

Shrimp Sushi Cones

Vinegar Water
1   cup (250 ml) cold water
1–2 tablespoons rice vinegar
Cones
4   nori sheets
1   recipe sushi rice (see pages 14–17)
1   pound (500 g) cooked shrimp, peeled
½   cup (120 ml) spicy mayonnaise
     (see page 119)
1   avocado, peeled, pitted, cut in thin strips
1   cucumber, cut lengthwise into thin strips
2   scallions (spring onions), trimmed and
     quartered lengthwise
     Sriracha sauce
4   tablespoons flying fish roe
2–3 tablespoons black sesame seeds
     Micro-cress, to garnish

• Prepare the vinegar water.

• Cut the nori sheets in half.

• Place a nori sheet shiny side down on a clean cutting board. Dip your hands into the vinegar water. Spread 1–2 tablespoons of sushi rice over half of the nori sheet.

• Spread the rice with mayonnaise. Lay pieces of shrimp, avocado, cucumber, and scallions diagonally across the rice.

• Roll up into cones following the instructions in the video or step by step. Repeat with the remaining ingredients.

• Spoon fish roe on to the ends, sprinkle with sesame seeds, and dab with Sriracha.

• Arrange on plates, garnish with extra mayonnaise, Sriracha, and cress, and serve.

Pressed Sushi

PRESSED SUSHI, also known as box sushi, is called *oshizushi* in Japanese. It is named for the oshibako box in which it is made.

2:59

OSHIZUSHI is traditionally made in a three-piece cypress wood box. If you are using a wooden box, soak it in cold water for 30 minutes before use. This will stop the rice from sticking to the box. Nowadays, many sushi molds are made of plastic and don't require soaking. A mold is handy if you make this type of sushi often, but it is not essential. You can also a pan with a removeable bottom, such as a springform cake pan. If using a cake pan, remove the base and place the pan on a clean dry chopping board. Line with plastic wrap and fill as directed in the recipe. Use the base to press down on the rice.

PRESSED SUSHI WITH MARINATED MACKEREL

2	(5-ounce/150-g) fillets of mackerel, with skin
½	cup (100 g) coarse sea salt
1	cup (250 ml) Japanese rice vinegar
¼	cup (60 ml) water
1	tablespoon sugar
1	tablespoon mirin
½	recipe sushi rice (see pages 14–17)
	Banana leaves to line the oshibako, and to garnish (optional)
	Wasabi paste
	Thinly sliced lemon and pickled ginger, to garnish
	Cucumber garnish (see pages 112–115)

OPPOSITE: PRESSED SUSHI WITH MARINATED MACKEREL

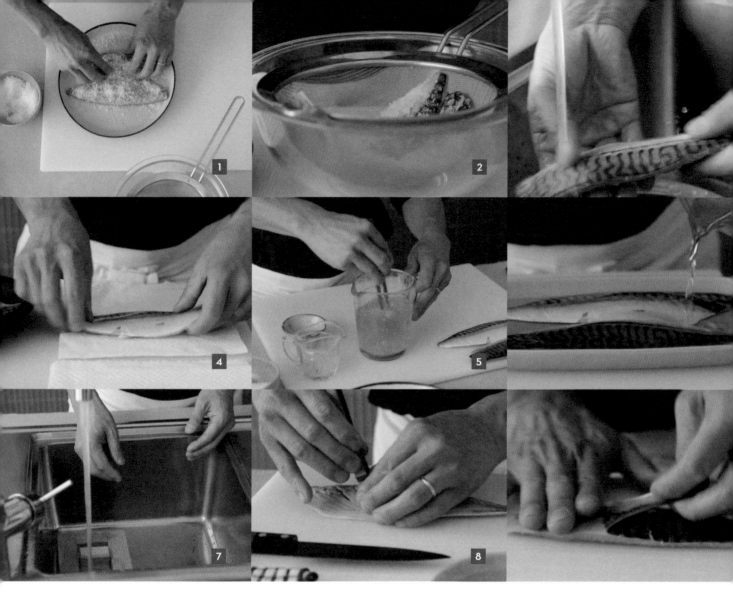

Pressed Sushi with Marinated Mackerel
Step by step

1. Lay the mackerel fillets in a shallow bowl and sprinkle with the salt. Gently rub the salt over the fillets.

2. Transfer to a colander and let drain for 3–4 hours.

3. Rinse carefully to remove excess salt.

4. Dry carefully with a clean kitchen cloth or paper towels.

5. Mix the rice vinegar, water, sugar, and mirin in a plastic bowl or pitcher (jug), stirring until the sugar is dissolved.

6. Place the mackerel in a shallow dish and pour the vinegar mixture over it. Let marinate for 1 hour. The flesh will turn very white.

7. If using a wooden sushi mold, soak it in cold water for 30 minutes.

8. Remove the fillets from the marinade and dry carefully on paper towels. Transfer the fillets to a chopping board. Trim the edges to even. Run your fingertips over the fish, feeling for bones. Use tweezers to remove.

9. Remove the thin outer layer of skin from the fish. Leave the iridescent underskin on.

10. Using a sharp knife, slice the mackerel fillets in half horizontally.

11. Trim the ends off the banana leaves to fit in the mold. Place a layer of banana leaves inside, or line with plastic wrap.

12. Trim half the mackerel fillets to fit the sushi mold. Place skin-side down in the mold.

13. Dab with wasabi. Top with half of the sushi rice and cover with more banana leaves (or plastic wrap).

14. Cover the mold with the lid and press to compact the sushi.

15. Carefully remove the sushi from the mold and place on a cutting board. Remove the banana leaves.

16. Garnish serving plates with pieces of banana leaf, if liked.

17. Cut the pressed sushi in half , then cut each half into three pieces. Repeat with the remaining ingredients.

18. Arrange on the plates. Garnish with the lemon, pickled ginger, and cucumber, and serve.

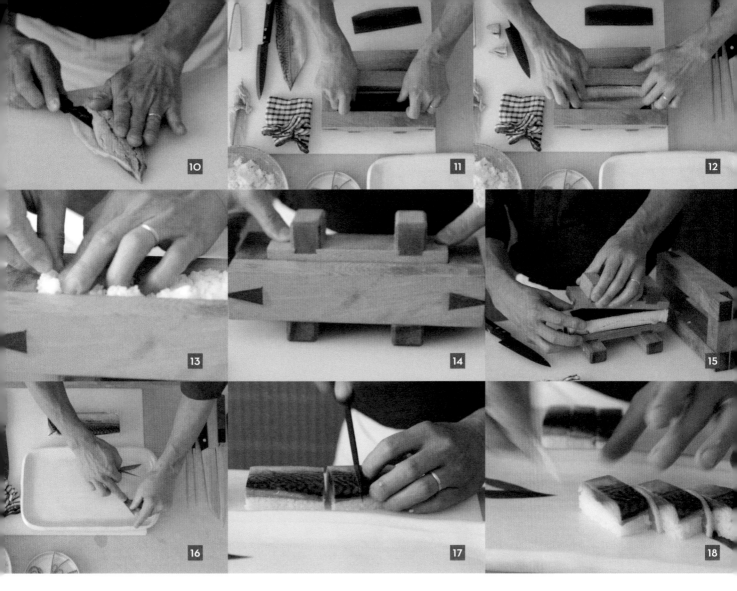

Yellowtail & Flying Fish Roe Pressed Sushi

½   recipe sushi rice (see pages 14–17)
8   ounces (250 g) sashimi-quality yellowtail, thinly sliced against the grain
2–3   tablespoons red or green flying fish roe (tobiko)
      Wasabi paste and pickled ginger, to garnish

• If using a wooden sushi mold, soak it in cold water for 30 minutes.

• Line the mold with plastic wrap (cling film).

• Arrange half the yellowtail in an even layer in the bottom of the mold.

• Spread evenly with half the fish roe. Top with half the rice.

• Cover the mold with the lid and press to compact the sushi.

• Carefully remove the sushi from the mold and place on a cutting board. Remove the plastic wrap.

• Cut the pressed sushi in half crosswise, then cut each half into three pieces. Repeat with the remaining ingredients.

• Arrange on serving plates. Garnish with pickled ginger and wasabi, and serve.

Smoked Salmon & Lime Pressed Sushi

½   recipe sushi rice (see pages 14–17)
1   unwaxed lime, with peel, halved and sliced paper thin + extra slices, to garnish
8   ounces (250 g) smoked salmon
Wasabi paste
Pickled ginger, to serve
Fresh green or red shiso (perilla) leaves, to garnish

• If using a wooden sushi mold, soak it in cold water for 30 minutes.

• Line the mold with plastic wrap (cling film).

• Line the sushi mold with slices of lime, overlapping the slices a little.

• Cover with half the smoked salmon in an even layer. Dab with wasabi and top with half of the sushi rice.

• Cover the mold with the lid and press to compact the sushi.

• Carefully remove the sushi from the mold and place on a cutting board. Remove the plastic wrap.

• Cut the pressed sushi in half crosswise, then cut each half into three pieces. Repeat with the remaining ingredients.

• Garnish serving plates with shiso leaves and extra slices of lime.

• Arrange the sushi on top, and serve.

OPPOSITE: SMOKED SALMON & LIME PRESSED SUSHI

Smoked Chicken & Apple Pressed Sushi

1   recipe sushi rice (see page 7)
6   ounces (180 g) thinly sliced smoked chicken (from the deli counter)
Sriracha sauce
1   large, organic Granny Smith apple, with peel, cored, and sliced paper thin
Half a fresh lemon
Seaweed salad, to serve

• If using a wooden sushi mold, soak it in cold water for 30 minutes.

• Line the mold with plastic wrap (cling film).

• Arrange half the chicken in an even layer in the bottom of the mold.

• Cover the chicken with a quarter of the rice. Top with an even layer of sliced apple and squeeze some lemon juice over the top (remove any pips).

• Cover the apple with another quarter of the rice.

• Cover the mold with the lid and press to compact the sushi.

• Carefully remove the sushi from the mold and place on a cutting board. Remove the plastic wrap.

• Cut the pressed sushi in half crosswise, then cut each half into three pieces. Repeat with the remaining ingredients.

• Arrange on serving plates, and serve with the seaweed.

Fresh Salmon Pressed Sushi with Nori & Fish Roe

1	nori sheet
10	ounces (300 g) sashimi-quality salmon, thinly sliced against the grain
½	recipe sushi rice (see pages 14–17)
2	tablespoons red or green flying fish roe (tobiko)
	Mayonnaise, to garnish

• If using a wooden sushi mold, soak it in cold water for 30 minutes. Line the mold with plastic wrap (cling film).

• Use a sharp knife or kitchen scissors to cut the nori into strips to fit the mold.

• Arrange half the salmon in an even layer in the bottom of the sushi mold.

• Spread with one-sixth of the rice. Cover with a strip of nori.

• Spread with one-sixth of the rice. Use a teaspoon to spread the rice with half the fish roe. Cover with a strip of nori and top with another sixth of the rice.

• Cover the mold with the lid and press to compact the sushi.

• Carefully remove the sushi from the mold and place on a cutting board. Remove the plastic wrap.

• Cut the pressed sushi in half crosswise, then cut each half into three pieces. Repeat with the remaining ingredients.

• Arrange on serving plates, garnish with the mayonnaise, and serve.

Nigiri

NIGIRIZUSHI means "hand-pressed" sushi. It is made by pressing a fistful of sushi rice into an oblong and draping it with a piece of fish or another topping.

NIGIRIZUSHI is fun to make although it can be more challenging than other types. A platter of nigiri makes an eyecatching and tasty appetizer and is perfect with predinner drinks. If making the fresh fish nigiri platter in the recipe shown here, you must find the very best quality fresh fish money can buy and be sure to serve it as soon as possible after making. It needs to be absolutely fresh.

MIXED SEAFOOD NIGIRI PLATTER

Vinegar Water

1	cup (250 ml) cold water
1–2	tablespoons rice vinegar

Nigiri

8	large (tiger) shrimp (prawn) tails
5	ounces (150 g) sashimi-grade albacore tuna
5	ounces (150 g) sashimi-grade sea bream
5	ounces (150 g) sashimi-grade salmon
1	recipe sushi rice (see pages 14–17)
1	nori sheet, cut into strips measuring about 1 x 3½ inches (2.5 x 8.5 cm)
	Wasabi paste
	Banana leaves and pickled ginger, to serve

OPPOSITE: MIXED SEAFOOD NIGIRI PLATTER

Mixed Seafood Nigiri Platter

Step by step

1. Vinegar Water: Mix the water and vinegar in a small bowl and set aside.

2. Use a toothpick to devein the shrimp, pulling the vein from the bellies and discarding it. Then press a toothpick through each shrimp from top to tail to prevent it from curling during cooking.

3. Bring a large pot of water to a gentle simmer over medium heat. Add the shrimp and simmer until pink, 2–3 minutes. Remove using chopsticks or tongs and place in a bowl of cold water until cool enough to handle.

4. Discard the toothpicks and remove the heads and shells from the shrimp.

5. Use a knife to make a slit up the center of the belly and open the shrimp out.

6. Lay all the fish on a clean chopping board. Thinly slice the tuna, salmon, and sea bream into pieces measuring about 1 x 2 inches (2.5 x 5 cm).

VARIATION   MAKES **ABOUT 20 PIECES**   PREPARATION **30 MINUTES + TIME FOR THE RICE**

Carpaccio Nigiri in Chicory Boats

Vinegar Water
1   cup (250 ml) cold water
1–2   tablespoons rice vinegar

Nigiri
20   small-to-medium chicory (witloof) leaves
2   nori sheets
7   ounces (200 g) top-quality steak (tenderloin is ideal), sliced about ⅛ inch (3 mm) thick
1   recipe sushi rice (see pages 14–17) Wasabi paste and pickled ginger, to serve

• Prepare the vinegar water.

• Set out the chicory leaves.

• Cut the nori sheets into strips about ½ inch (1 cm) wide.

• Cut the beef into rectangles that will fit over the chicory leaves.

• Dip your hands into the vinegar water. Squeeze a handful of rice into an oblong that will fit snugly into a chicory leaf.

• Place the rice in the leaf and dab with a little wasabi. Cover with a piece of beef.

• Wrap a strip of nori around the middle, sticking the ends together with a little water, and tucking them underneath the chicory leaf. Repeat with the remaining ingredients.

• Arrange on serving plates, garnish with ginger and wasabi, and serve.

7. Dip your hands into the vinegar water, and squeeze a large tablespoon of the sushi rice gently in the palm of one hand into an oblong.

8. Dab a piece of tuna with wasabi and fit it over the rice, squeezing and turning to stick the tuna to the rice. Repeat with the remaining slices of tuna, salmon, and sea bream.

9. Squeeze more rice into an oblong. Pick up a shrimp and place the rice on it, squeezing, pressing, and turning together as before.

10. Wrap a piece of nori around the shrimp nigiri, squeezing the ends together under the rice to make it stick. Repeat with all the remaining rice and shrimp.

11. If liked, cut diamond-shapes out of a banana leaf and use it to decorate a large serving platter.

12. Arrange all the nigiri decoratively on the platter, and serve.

VARIATION   MAKES **16–24 PIECES**   PREPARATION **45 MINUTES + TIME FOR THE RICE**   COOKING **15 MINUTES**

Bell Pepper Nigiri

Vinegar Water
1   cup (250 ml) cold water
1–2   tablespoons rice vinegar

Nigiri
2   small red bell peppers (capsicums), seeded and cut into 4–6 strips
1   small yellow bell peppers (capsicums), seeded and cut into 4–6 strips
1   recipe sushi rice (see pages 14–17)
     Wasabi paste
2   nori sheets
     Wakame (seaweed), to serve

• Prepare the vinegar water.

• Preheat a grill pan (griddle) or overhead broiler (grill) in the oven.

• Grill the bell peppers until the skins are charred. Place in a plastic food bag and let sweat for 10 minutes. Remove from the bag and peel off all the chared skin.

• Slice the bell peppers into 1½ x 2½-inch (4 x 6-cm) strips.

• Dip your hands into the vinegar water. Squeeze a handful of rice into an oblong and dab the top with wasabi.

• Drape a piece of bell pepper over the rice. Wrap a strip of nori around the middle, sticking the ends together with a little water, and tucking them underneath. Repeat with the remaining ingredients.

• Arrange on serving plates, garnish with the wakame, and serve.

Omelet Nigiri

NIGIRI can also be topped with a special type of Japanese omelet, called *tamago*.

2:18

UNLIKE French omelets which are folded after cooking, Japanese omelets are rolled while in the frying pan. The result is a kind of egg roll. They are made in rectangular pans called makiyakinabe.

JAPANESE OMELET NIGIRI

Vinegar Water

1	cup (250 ml) cold water
1–2	tablespoons rice vinegar

Nigiri

2	nori sheets
4	large eggs + 1 large egg yolk
2	tablespoons sugar
1	teaspoon soy sauce
1	tablespoon butter
	Wasabi paste
½	recipe sushi rice (see pages 14–17)
	Salad greens, cilantro (coriander), and sliced radish, to garnish

OPPOSITE: JAPANESE OMELET NIGIRI

Japanese Omelet Nigiri
Step by step

You can buy a tamagoyaki (Japanese omelet pan) from well stocked kitchen supply stores or from many online suppliers.

1. Place the omelet pan over medium-low heat.
2. Vinegar Water: Mix the water and vinegar in a small bowl and set aside.
3. Cut the nori sheets in half then cut into ¼-inch (5-mm) wide strips.
4. Combine the eggs and egg yolk in a bowl and stir with chopsticks or whisk until smooth. Add the sugar and soy sauce, stirring until well mixed.
5. Pour the egg mixture into a pitcher (jug).
6. Add the butter to the omelet pan, using chopsticks to distribute evenly in the pan.
7. Pour the egg mixture into the pan. Tilt the pan so that the egg mixture covers the base in an even layer.
8. When the egg looks opaque and you can get a spatula under it without tearing the omelet, use chopsticks to begin rolling it up.
9. Keep rolling the egg mixture.
10. When the egg is golden brown and loosely rolled at the end of the pan, tip it out onto a clean dry chopping board.
11. Slice into 1½ x 2½-inch (4 x 6-cm) strips.
12. Dip your hands into the vinegar water, and squeeze a large tablespoon of the sushi rice gently in the palm of one hand into an oblong. Repeat with all the rice.
13. Dab a each rice oblong with some wasabi and place a piece of omelet on top.
14. Wrap a strip of nori around the middle, sticking the ends together with a little water, and tucking them underneath. Repeat with the remaining rice oblongs and omelet.
15. Arrange the nigiri on serving plates, garnish with the salad greens, cilantro, and radish, and serve.

Warship Sushi

GUNKANMAKI, or warship sushi, are a special
form of hand-pressed nigiri.

MIXED FISH ROE WARSHIP SUSHI

Vinegar Water

1	cup (250 ml) cold water
1–2	tablespoons rice vinegar

Warships

4	nori sheets
1	recipe sushi rice (see pages 14–17)
	Wasabi paste
4	ounces (120 g) green flying fish roe (green tobiko)
4	ounces (120 g) salmon roe
4	ounces (120 g) caviar (black fish roe)
	Pickled ginger, to serve
	Soy sauce, to serve

*WARSHIP SUSHI is made by first
preparing strips of nori and
wrapping them around hand-
pressed oblongs of sushi rice.
The strips of nori should be slightly
taller than the rice leaving a space
for the filling. Fish roe is a
traditional filling, but you can fill*
*the tiny vessels with any soft or
finely chopped ingredient, including
tuna salad, corn and mayonnaise
mixtures, and many others.
Gunkanmaki sushi was invented at
the Ginza Kyubey restaurant in
Tokyo in 1941.*

OPPOSITE: MIXED FISH ROE WARSHIP SUSHI

Mixed Fish Roe Warship Sushi
Step by step

1. Vinegar Water: Mix the water and vinegar in a small bowl and set aside.
2. Cut each nori sheet into six equal strips.
3. Dip your hands into the vinegar water and squeeze a large tablespoon of the sushi rice gently in the palm of one hand into an oblong. Repeat with all the rice.
4. Dab the tops of the rice oblongs with wasabi paste.
5. Take a strip of nori and wrap it around an oblong of rice.
6. Place 1–2 grains of rice on one end of the nori strip and press it against the other end. The rice will help stick the nori together in a firm ring.
7. The sides of the nori should come slightly above the rice, leaving a hollow space for the filling. Repeat with the remaining rice and nori strips.
8. Use a teaspoon to fill the tops of the warships with the different types of fish roe.
9. Arrange the warship sushi pieces on serving plates.
10. Garnish with pickled ginger and wasabi paste, and serve with the soy sauce.

Teriyaki Chicken Warships

Vinegar Water
1   cup (250 ml) cold water
1–2   tablespoons rice vinegar

Warships
4   nori sheets
¼   cup (60 ml) dark soy sauce
¼   cup (60 ml) saké
2   teaspoons sugar
14   ounces (400 g) boneless, skinless
          chicken breast, sliced into thin strips
1   recipe sushi rice (sees page 14–17)
          Sweet chili sauce, to serve
          Snipped fresh chives
          Spicy mayonnaise (see page 119),
          to serve
          Capers, to garnish

• Prepare the vinegar water.

• Cut each nori sheet into six equal strips.

• Combine the soy sauce, saké, and sugar
in a small bowl and mix well.

• Place the chicken in a large bowl and
pour the soy sauce mixture over the top.
Mix gently to coat all over and set aside to
marinate for 30 minutes.

• Preheat a grill pan (griddle) or frying pan
and cook the chicken until tender, 5–7
minutes.

• Dip your hands into the vinegar water,
and squeeze large tablespoons of rice into
oblongs. Repeat with all the rice.

• Wrap the strips of nori around the rice
following the instructions in the video or
step by step.

• Use a teaspoon to fill the tops of the
warships with the chicken mixture.

• Arrange the warship sushi pieces on a
serving platter. Garnish half the warships
with a dab of sweet chili sauce and a
sprinkling of chives.

• Garnish the remaining warships with a
dab of spicy mayonnaise and 1–2 capers,
and serve.

Shrimp Salad Warships

Vinegar Water
1   cup (250 ml) cold water
1–2   tablespoons rice vinegar

Warships
4   nori sheets
4   tablespoons frozen peas
1   carrot, cut into tiny cubes
          Salt
5   ounces (150 g) small, peeled cooked
          shrimp (prawns),coarsely chopped
⅓   cup (90 ml) spicy mayonnaise
          (see page 119)
1   recipe sushi rice (sees page 14–17)
          Microcress, thinly sliced carrot, and
          sesame seeds, to garnish

• Prepare the vinegar water.

• Cut each nori sheet into six equal strips.

• Cook the peas and carrots in a small pot
of lightly salted boiling water until just
tender, 3–4 minutes. Drain well.

• Place the shrimp in a small bowl. Add the
mayonnaise, peas and carrots. Mix well.

• Dip your hands in the vinegar water, and
squeeze the rice gently into oblongs.

• Wrap the nori around the rice as shown in
the video or step by step.

• Use a teaspoon to fill the warships with
the shrimp filling.

• Arrange the sushi on serving plates. Top
with the cress, garnish with the carrot and
sesame, and serve.

Sushi Balls

THESE attractive rounds are known as *temarizushi*, which means "hand-ball sushi" in Japanese.

MIXED SUSHI BALL PLATTER

Vinegar Water

1   cup (250 ml) cold water

1–2 tablespoons rice vinegar

Sushi Balls

1   recipe sushi rice
     see pages 14–17)

6   ounces (180 g) sashimi-quality
     sea bream fillet

16   shiso leaves

2   teaspoons black sesame seeds

16   small uncooked shrimp (prawns)
     Wasabi paste (optional)

2   ounces (60 g) red flying fish roe
     Thinly sliced lemon and chives,
     to garnish

HAND-BALL SUSHI is easier to make than other hand-pressed sushi and a platter of these delicacies will be a sure success as an appetizer or with predinner drinks. As usual, you can prepare them with a variety of toppings. Here you will learn the basic technique and a couple of variations. We suggest that you serve them with some nigiri and sushi rolls for maximum effect.

OPPOSITE: MIXED SUSHI BALL PLATTER

Mixed Sushi Ball Platter
Step by step

1. Vinegar Water: Mix the water and vinegar in a small bowl and set aside.

2. Use a toothpick to devein the shrimp.

Then press a toothpick through each shrimp from top to tail to prevent it from curling during cooking.

3. Bring a large pot of water to a gentle simmer over medium heat. Add the shrimp and simmer until pink, 2–3 minutes. Remove using chopsticks or tongs and place in a bowl of ice water until cool enough to handle.

4. Drain and pull out the toothpicks.

Remove the heads and shells. Dry on paper towels.

5. Cut the shrimp in half crosswise. Then cut down the center lengthwise. Open out and cut in half lengthwise again, on both sides. Set aside.

6. Use a sharp knife to slice the sea bream very thinly across the fillet. You will need 16 small very thin slices (about 1½ inches/4 cm square).

VARIATION   MAKES **ABOUT 30 BALLS**   PREPARATION **30 MINUTES + TIME FOR THE RICE**

Vegetarian Sushi Balls

Vinegar Water
1   cup (250 ml) cold water
1–2   tablespoons rice vinegar

Sushi Balls
2   medium carrots, finely grated
6   scallions (spring onions), finely chopped
1   recipe sushi rice (see pages 14–17)
¼   cup toasted white sesame seeds
¼   cup toasted black sesame seeds

Wasabi Ginger Sauce
1   tablespoon wasabi powder
¼   cup (60 ml) water
1   clove garlic
1   tablespoon finely chopped fresh ginger
2   tablespoons peanut oil
3   tablespoons rice vinegar
⅓   cup (90 ml) soy sauce

• Prepare the vinegar water.

• Stir the carrots and scallions into the rice.

• Cut 30 pieces of plastic wrap (cling film) into 6-inch (15-cm) squares.

• Place a piece of plastic wrap on a clean dry chopping board.

• Dip your fingers into the vinegar water. Squeeze 1 tablespoon of rice mixture into a ball. Place in the center of the plastic.

• Pull the corners of the plastic around the rice as shown in the video and step by step. Repeat with the remaining rice.

• Unwrap the balls and roll half in the white sesame seeds and half in the black.

• Mix all the sauce ingredients in a bowl. Serve with the sushi balls.

7. Cut 30 pieces of plastic wrap (cling film) into 6-inch (15-cm) squares.

8. Place a piece of plastic wrap on a clean dry chopping board. Place a piece of sliced shrimp in the center. Dab with a little wasabi paste, if liked.

9. Dip your fingers into the vinegar water. Take up a small handful of rice (about 1 tablespoon), and place on the shrimp.

10. Pull the four corners of the plastic wrap around the rice and shrimp ball, twisting to compact the rice and press it into a small firm ball. Repeat with the remaining shrimp.

11. Place a slice of sea bream in the center of a piece of plastic wrap. Top with a piece of shiso. Dip your fingers into the vinegar water. Take up a small handful of rice (about 1 tablespoon), and place on the shiso.

Pull the plastic around the fish and rice ball and press it into a small firm ball. Repeat with the remaining sea bream and rice.

12. Arrange the balls on serving plates. Decorate the tops of the shrimp balls with fish roe and the sea bream balls with sesame seeds. Garnish with the lemon and chives, and serve.

VARIATION   MAKES **ABOUT 30 BALLS**   PREPARATION **30 MINUTES + TIME FOR THE RICE**

Avocado Sushi Balls

Vinegar Water
1   cup (250 ml) cold water
1–2   tablespoons rice vinegar

Sushi Balls
3   tablespoons black sesame seeds
3   tablespoons white sesame seeds
3   tablespoons toasted almond slivers, chopped
4   scallions (spring onions), very finely chopped
1   recipe sushi rice (see pages 14–17)
2   avocados, peeled, pitted, halved, and very thinly sliced
    Wasabi paste
    Shiso (perilla) leaves, to garnish

• Prepare the vinegar water.

• Stir the sesame seeds, almonds, and scallions into the sushi rice.

• Cut 30 pieces of plastic wrap (cling film) into 6-inch (15-cm) squares.

• Place a piece of plastic on a clean dry chopping board. Place 4–5 slices of avocado, slightly overlapping, in the center.

• Dip your fingers into the vinegar water. Squeeze 1 tablespoon of rice mixture into a ball. Place on the avocado.

• Pull the corners of the plastic around the rice as shown in the video and step by step. Repeat with the remaining ingredients.

• Arrange the rice balls on serving plates, garnish with the shiso, and serve.

Stuffed Squid Sushi

THIS DISH is known as *ika meshi*, which means "squid rice" in Japanese.

STUFFED SQUID SUSHI

2	medium squid, cleaned
3	tablespoons saké
3	tablespoons rice vinegar
2	tablespoons sugar
1	tablespoon mirin
2	tablespoons soy sauce
2	ounces (60 g) ground (minced) chicken breast
1	tablespoon peeled and finely chopped fresh ginger
½	recipe sushi rice (see pages 14–17)
	Wakame and salad greens, to garnish

THIS is the best way to enjoy squid with sushi rice and these rolls are not too difficult to prepare. Take care not to overcook the squid as it will become rubbery and tough if you leave it in the simmering water for too long; 1–2 minutes will be plenty. The meat will turn white when ready. If liked, you can change the filling by adding sesame seeds or other flavors.

OPPOSITE: STUFFED SQUID SUSHI

Stuffed Squid
Sushi Rolls
Step by step

*Most fish vendors sell squid that has
already been cleaned but it is not
difficult to clean at home. Use a sharp
knife to cut off the tentacles below the
eyes. Flip the tentacles back and
squeeze out and discard the beak. Trim
off the flaps on the sides of the body.
Squeeze out the viscera, including the
plastic-like skeleton, or "quill."*

1. Rinse the squid thoroughly under cold running water.

2. Remove the squid skins by pulling down and peeling them off the bodies.

3. Trim the ends off the squid and set the bodies aside on a plate.

4. Trim the tentacles and flaps and add to the plate with the bodies.

5. Bring a pan half full with water to a boil and add 1 tablespoon each of saké and rice vinegar. Add the squid bodies and simmer for 1–2 minutes. Do not overcook, as the squid will become rubbery.

6. Remove the squid and place in ice water to cool. Drain and place in a shallow bowl. Drizzle with the remaining rice vinegar.

7. Finely chop the tentacles and trimmings.

8. Combine the remaining 2 tablespoons of saké, the sugar, mirin, and soy sauce in a saucepan over medium heat and bring to a boil. Add the chicken, the chopped squid, and the ginger. Stir with a fork until the meat turns white.

9. Using a slotted spoon, transfer the cooked meat mixture to another bowl, leaving the juice in the saucepan.

10. Boil the juices over high heat until thickened, 1–2 minutes.

11. Stir the meat back in to absorb the juices, then remove from the heat.

12. Stir the squid mixture into the sushi rice.

13. Stuff each squid with the rice mixture.

14. Transfer to a clean dry chopping board and cut each squid into four to six even slices.

15. Arrange the squid sushi on serving plates, garnish with the wakame and salad greens, and serve.

Scattered Sushi, Edo Style

SCATTERED SUSHI is the easiest type to prepare. When prepared Edo-style, the toppings are artfully scattered over a bed of sushi rice.

4:00

EDO is the ancient name for the city of Tokyo. Our recipe, with a mixture of raw and cooked seafood, mushrooms, and omelet, is a classic one, but you can vary it to suit your tastes or the ingredients you have on hand.

This recipe calls for dashi stock which can be made from special dashi stock granules or powders. Just simmer the granules or powder in boiling water for the time indicated on the package.

SCATTERED SUSHI, EDO STYLE

16	dried shiitake mushrooms
1	recipe sushi rice (see pages 14–17)
1	cup (250 ml) dashi stock
½	cup (120 ml) dark soy sauce
¼	cup (60 ml) mirin
4	tablespoons (60 ml) saké
2	tablespoons sugar
4	medium carrots, cut lengthwise into long strips
6	large shrimp (prawns)
6	pieces squid, about 3 inches (8 cm) square
2	large eggs + 4 large egg yolks
12	ounces (350 g) sashimi-quality fresh tuna
6	snow peas (mangetout), parboiled, and thinly sliced
	Watercress sprigs and sesame seeds, to garnish

OPPOSITE: SCATTERED SUSHI, EDO STYLE

Scattered Sushi Edo-Style
Step by step

1. Place the dried shiitake mushrooms in a bowl and cover with warm water. Let soak until softened, about 4 hours. Drain.

2. Heat ½ cup (120 ml) of dashi stock with ¼ cup (60 ml) of soy sauce, the mirin, and 2 tablespoons of saké in a small saucepan over medium heat. Add the mushrooms and simmer for 15 minutes. Remove from the heat and let rest in the liquid for 2 hours.

3. Drain, and cut the best-looking twelve mushrooms in half and set aside.

4. Chop the remaining mushrooms.

5. Heat the remaining dashi with the remaining soy sauce, remaining saké, and the sugar in a small saucepan over medium heat. Add the carrots and simmer until just tender, 7–8 minutes.

6. Drain and let cool.

7. Use a toothpick to devein the shrimp. Then press a toothpick through each shrimp from top to tail to prevent it from curling during cooking.

8. Cook the shrimp in a pot of boiling water until pink, 2–3 minutes. Transfer to a bowl of ice water and let cool.

9. Drain and dry on paper towels. Remove the heads, then slit in half lengthwise by cutting them open down the underside of the bellies.

10. Score the outside of the squid diagonally at ¼-inch (5-mm) intervals.

11. Dip the squid pieces into boiling water for 20–30 seconds, until they curl.

12. Plunge into ice water. Drain.

13. Beat the eggs with the yolks and strain.

14. Make a large thin omelet. When cool, fold and cut into thin strips.

15. Toss the sushi rice with the chopped mushrooms.

16. Cut the tuna against the grain into slices about ¼ inch (5 mm) thick.

17. Put the rice in a large serving platter or divide into four to six portions on individual serving plates. Top with the egg strips, mushroom halves, shrimp, squid, tuna, carrots, and snow peas.

18. Garnish with sprigs of watercress and sesame seeds, and serve.

SERVES **4-6**   PREPARATION **20 MINUTES + TIME FOR THE RICE**

Tuna & Salmon Scattered Sushi

2   tablespoons toasted white sesame seeds
1   recipe sushi rice (see pages 14–17)
4   ounces (120 g) sashimi-grade fresh salmon, thinly sliced
4   ounces (120 g) sashimi-grade fresh tuna, thinly sliced
2   teaspoons flying fish roe
2   tablespoons wakame seaweed
1   tablespoon pickled ginger
    Wasabi paste, to serve
    Soy sauce, to serve

· Stir the toasted sesame seeds into the sushi rice.

· Divide the rice evenly among four to six serving bowls.

· Arrange slices of salmon, tuna, flying fish roe, wakamae, and pickled ginger on top.

· Serve with some wasabi and soy sauce.

Scattered Sushi, Kansi Style

WHEN preparing Kansi-style sushi the fillings are stirred into the rice before serving.

KANSI-STYLE SCATTERED SUSHI is one of the simplest forms of sushi, and perfect for family suppers and casual gatherings with friends. Once you have mastered the basic recipe, you can be adventurous with this style, trying out various combinations of ingredients to suit your own tastes.

SCATTERED SUSHI, KANSI STYLE

1	(2-inch/5-cm) piece ginger, finely chopped
2	cloves garlic, finely chopped
1	scallion (spring onion), finely chopped
1	tablespoon coriander seeds, crushed
	Salt and freshly ground black pepper
4	tablespoons (60 ml) saké
1	pound (500 g) salmon fillets, skin removed
1	small sweet pineapple
1	tablespoon butter
1	tablespoon red pepper flakes
1	avocado, peeled, pitted, and diced
1	small cucumber, diced
1	large tomato, diced
1	small bunch fresh cilantro (coriander), coarsely chopped
1	recipe sushi rice (see pages 14–17)

OPPOSITE: SCATTERED SUSHI, KANSI STYLE

Scattered Sushi, Kansi Style
Step by step

1. Combine the ginger, garlic, scallion, coriander, salt, and pepper in a shallow bowl.

2. Add with saké and salmon. Cover the salmon with the mixture and set aside for 1 hour.

3. Peel the pineapple and dice the flesh. Set aside.

4. Melt 1 tablespoon of butter in a medium pan until bubbling.

5. Add the red pepper flakes, pineapple, and 2 tablespoons of the saké marinade. Cook down until all the liquid has evaporated. Set aside.

6. Heat a frying pan over high heat. Add the remaining tablespoon of butter and sear the salmon in the pan for 1–2 minutes.

7. Remove from the pan and set aside to cool a little.

8. Stir the avocado, cucumber, tomato, and cilantro into the sushi rice.

9. Slice the salmon.

10. Divide the rice salad evenly among six to eight serving plates. Top with pieces of salmon and the pineapple mixture, and serve immediately.

Spring Festival Scattered Sushi

Radish Petals
4   radishes, trimmed
2   tablespoons rice vinegar
2   tablespoons sugar

Egg Petals
1   large egg, beaten
    Salt
½   teaspoon cornstarch (cornflour),
    mixed with 1 teaspoon water
    Sunflower oil, for frying

Vegetables
6   dried shiitake mushrooms
5   tablespoons sugar
2½   tablespoons mirin
¼   cup (60 ml) chicken stock
1   teaspoon soy sauce
1   small carrot, sliced into 1-inch
    (2.5-cm) matchsticks
8   snow peas (mangetout), trimmed
4   ounces (120 g) cod fillet
1   tablespoon saké
8   ounces (250 g) small shrimp (prawns),
    peeled and lightly cooked
3   tablespoons white sesame seeds,
    lightly toasted in a dry frying pan
1   recipe sushi rice (see pages 14–17)

• Radish Petals: Cut tiny wedges out of each radish, then slice crosswise to form 5–6 petal shapes.

• Combine the vinegar and sugar in a bowl and stir until the sugar has dissolved. Add the radish slices and marinate for 6 hours, or overnight.

• Egg Petals: Mix the egg in a bowl with a pinch of salt and the cornstarch mixture.

• Heat a small frying pan, brush with oil, add the egg mixture, and cook until set. Using small flower-shaped molds or cookie cutters, cut out flower shapes from the omelet.

• Vegetables: Soak the shiitake in warm water for 4 hours.

• Drain, reserving the soaking liquid. Discard the stems and thinly slice the caps.

• Combine the shiitake, ⅓ cup (90 ml) of soaking liquid, 2 tablespoons of sugar, and mirin in a pan over low heat and simmer until the liquid evaporates.

• Put the chicken stock in a saucepan, add ½ teaspoon of sugar, a pinch of salt, and the carrot. Bring to a boil then simmer until just soft, 2–3 minutes. Let cool in the liquid.

• Blanch the snow peas in salted water. Slice diagonally.

• Simmer the cod in boiling water for 3–4 minutes, then drain. Return to a dry saucepan, add the saké, remaining sugar, and salt. Use a fork to finely flake over low heat.

• Stir the shiitake, carrot, snow peas, fish, shrimp, and sesame seeds into the rice. Top with the radish and egg, and serve.

Easy Scattered Sushi

2   cups (300 g) frozen peas
1   cup (100 g) green beans, sliced
    Handful snow peas (mangetout), sliced
1   small yellow summer squash
    or 1 medium zucchini (courgette),
    thinly sliced
3   large eggs
⅛   teaspoon salt
⅛   teaspoon sugar
1   tablespoon peanut oil
1   medium carrot, grated
1   small cucumber, peeled, seeded, and
    grated
2   scallions (spring onions), thinly sliced
4   tablespoons pickled ginger
3   tablespoons sesame seeds, toasted
1   recipe sushi rice (see pages 14–17)

• Combine the peas, green beans, snow peas, and summer squash in a steamer and steam until just tender, about 5 minutes.

• Whisk the eggs in a medium bowl with the salt and sugar.

• Heat the oil in a large frying pan and pour in the egg mixture, swirling to cover the pan in an even layer. Cook until firm.

• Slip the omelet out of the pan onto a chopping board. Roll up loosely and coarsely chop.

• Add the omelet and all the other ingredients to the rice and mix gently.

• Transfer to a serving bowl, and serve warm or at room temperature.

Tofu Pouch Sushi

THIS SUSHI is made by stuffing sushi rice and filling into special fried tofu pouches.

INARIZUSHI is named in honor of one of the principal Shinto gods, Inari, who is believed to be very fond of fried tofu. Inarizushi is thought to have been invented in 1853. The tofu pouches, called aburaage, can be bought at Asian food markets or from online suppliers. You can also find the tofu pouches already prepared and cut in half, ready for stuffing with the sushi rice. They are usually in a can. We prefer to prepare them ourselves, even though it does take a little extra time and skill.

SPICY SHRIMP INARI

Tofu Pouches

6	tofu pouches (aburaage)
1½	cups (375 ml) dashi stock (see page 76)
3	tablespoons brown sugar
2	tablespoons saké
2	tablespoons mirin
4	tablespoons (60 ml) soy sauce

Filling

1	pound (500 g) shrimp (prawns), peeled and deveined
⅓	cup (90 ml) mayonnaise
1–2	tablespoons Sriracha sauce, or to taste
1–2	tablespoons fresh cilanto (coriander)
1	recipe sushi rice (see pages 14–17)

OPPOSITE: SPICY SHRIMP INARI

Spicy Shrimp Inari
Step by step

1. Vinegar water: mix the water and vinegar in a small bowl. Set aside.

2. Blanch the tofu pouches in a medium pot of boiling water for 2 minutes.

3. Drain well and dry on paper towels to remove the oil.

4. Place the dashi stock in a medium pot over medium-high heat and bring to a boil. Add the brown sugar, saké, mirin, and soy sauce, then reduce the heat to a gentle simmer.

5. Add the tofu pouches and simmer for 10 minutes. Remove the pan from the heat and let the pouches cool in the liquid.

6. Remove from the pot. Drain on paper towels, squeezing out the stock.

7. Cut in half to make 12 pouches.

8. Cook the shrimp in gently simmering water until pink, 2–3 minutes.

9. Scoop out with a slotted spoon and place in a bowl of ice water. Drain and dry on paper towels.

10. Coarsely chop the shrimp and place in a bowl.

11. Stir in the mayonnaise and enough Sriracha to make a spicy sauce.

12. Dip your fingers into the vinegar water. Take up handfuls of the sushi rice and squeeze gently into oblongs.

13. Tuck the rice oblongs into the prepared tofu pouches, pressing down to make room for the filling at the top.

14. Spoon the shrimp mixture into the top of the tofu pouches.

15. Arrange the filled inari on serving plates, top with the cilantro, and serve.

VARIATION SERVES **4–6** PREPARATION **30 MINUTES** + TIME FOR THE RICE & TO PREPARE THE INARI POUCHES COOKING **3–4 MINUTES**

Mushroom Inari

6	tofu pouches (aburaage)
24	shiitake mushroom caps, thinly sliced
8	tablespoons (120 ml) soy sauce
1	recipe sushi rice (see pages 14–17)

• Prepare the tofu pouches following the instructions in the video or step by step photography. Set aside until ready to fill.

• Combine the mushrooms and 3 tablespoons of the soy sauce in a medium frying pan over medium heat. Cook until softened, 3–4 minutes.

• Stir the mushroom and soy sauce mixture into the rice.

• Use a teaspoon to tightly pack the inari pouches with the rice mixture.

• Top each one with a slice of mushroom.

• Arrange on plates and serve, with the remaining soy sauce for dipping.

VARIATION SERVES **4–6** PREPARATION **30 MINUTES** + TIME FOR THE RICE & TO PREPARE THE INARI POUCHES COOKING **15 MINUTES**

Quinoa Inari

6	tofu pouches (aburaage)
1¼	cups (250 g) rainbow quinoa
2½	cups (625 ml) water
⅓	cup (90 ml) rice vinegar
2	tablespoons brown sugar
1	teaspoon salt
1½	tablespoons black sesame seeds
5	scallions (spring onions), 3 finely chopped and 2 shredded, to garnish

• Prepare the tofu pouches following the instructions in the video or step by step photography. Set aside until ready to fill.

• Rinse the quinoa in a colander under cold running water until the water runs clear.

• Place the quinoa in a medium pan with the water and bring to a boil. Simmer until all the water is absorbed and the quinoa is tender, about 15 minutes. Transfer to a shallow bowl.

• Combine the vinegar, sugar, and salt in a small bowl and stir until the sugar is dissolved.

• Pour the vinegar mixture over the quinoa, then mix gently with a wooden spoon until cooled and well combined.

• Mix in the sesame seeds and finely chopped scallions.

• Use a teaspoon to tightly pack the inari pouches with the quinoa mixture.

• Garnish the tops of the inari with the shredded scallions.

• Arrange on plates, and serve.

Moneybag Sushi

THESE attractive little parcels are made by folding a thin omelet around the rice filling and tying the top with a chive.

2:43

MONEYBAG SUSHI, or chakin-zushi or fukusa-zushi as it is known in Japan, is a pouch sushi (like inari), but in this case the pouch is made from a very thin omelet instead of fried tofu. In Japan, a "chakin" is a linen cloth used for purifying tea towels during the tea ceremony, while a "fukusa" is a square of silk

used by courtiers in the Heian period to wrap up gifts or precious objects. To a western eye, these little sushi look like old-fashioned moneybags with a drawstring top, hence our name. You can vary the filling inside the bags, but don't make it too bulky or heavy as the delicate omelet may break.

MONEYBAG SUSHI

Vinegar Water

1	cup (250 ml) cold water
1–2	tablespoons rice vinegar

Moneybags

5	dried shiitake mushrooms
1	tablespoon mirin
1½	tablespoons cornstarch (cornflour)
¼	cup (60 ml) water
4	large eggs + 4 large egg yolks
1	teaspoon salt
4	tablespoons (60 ml) vegetable oil
3	tablespoons black sesame seeds
½	recipe sushi rice (sees page 14–17)
	Fresh chives, to tie the moneybags

OPPOSITE: MONEYBAG SUSHI

Moneybag Sushi
Step by step

*This eyecatching sushi takes some skill
and practise to make. We advise you to
try it out a few times before inviting
friends to a feast!*

1. Soak the mushrooms in 1 cup (250 ml) of warm water for 4 hours.

2. Transfer to a small saucepan with the soaking water. Place over medium heat and bring to a boil. Stir in the mirin.

3. Remove from the heat and let cool in the liquid in a bowl.

4. Remove the mushrooms from the liquid and slice thinly.

5. Put the cornstarch in a small bowl and stir in the water.

6. Add the eggs, egg yolks, and salt and stir well.

7. Heat 1 tablespoon of oil in a 7-inch (18-cm) frying pan. Add enough of the egg mixture to coat the bottom of the pan. Tilt the pan to spread evenly and cook over medium heat until just set.

8. Turn the omelet and cook the other side. Remove from the pan and place on a plate. Cook the rest of the egg batter in the same way. You will get eight to ten thin omelets.

9. Toast the sesame seeds in a small frying pan over medium heat until crisp, 2–3 minutes.

10. Stir the sesame seeds and mushrooms into the sushi rice.

11. Dip your fingers into the vinegar water. Take a handful of the rice mixture and squeeze into a ball. Place in the center of an omelet.

12. Carefully draw the edges of the omelet up around the ball of rice, bringing them together at the top in the shape of an old-fashioned moneybag.

13. Tie the tops with chives.

14. Repeat with the remaining ingredients, until all the omelets and rice mixture are used.

15. Arrange on plates, and serve.

Children's Sushi

THE SIMPLE recipes in this chapter are suitable for you to prepare with your children giving a helping hand.

SUSHI usually looks enticing and children are naturally drawn to it, although some may find many of the flavors a little too "grown-up" for their still-developing taste buds. Here we have tried to create attractive shapes and colors, with blander or less unusual flavors. Sushi is generally very healthy and it is a good idea to encourage even young children to try all the dishes; many will surprise you by enjoying even the more sophisticated flavors. If not, they will love these and will not be discouraged from trying more adventurous dishes as they grow.

CHILDREN'S MIXED SUSHI

1	recipe sushi rice (sees page 14–17)

Gold Star Sushi

2	teaspoons vegetable oil
2	large eggs
1	tablespoon milk
1	tablespoon sugar

Green Leaf Sushi

1	cup (150 g) frozen peas
2	teaspoons sugar
	Sea salt flakes

Pink Heart Sushi

2	thin slices smoked salmon (or ham)

White Knight Sushi

1	cucumber
1	teaspoon white sesame seeds
	Tiny bunch microcress leaves

OPPOSITE: CHILDREN'S MIXED SUSHI

Children's Sushi
Step by step

1. Divide the rice into four equal portions.

2. Gold Star Sushi: Heat the oil in a small omelet pan over medium heat. Beat the eggs, milk, and sugar in a small bowl and pour into the pan.

3. Stir quickly with chopsticks and cook to make soft scrambled eggs. Remove from the pan and set aside to cool.

4. Dip a star-shaped cookie cutter in water. Place on a clean dry cutting board and fill with rice. Press down with your fingers to compact the rice.

5. Spoon some scrambled egg on top and carefully remove the cutter. Repeat with a quarter of the rice.

6. Green Tree Sushi: Bring a small pan of salted water to a boil and add the peas. Simmer until tender, 2–3 minutes.

7. Drain and dry on a clean kitchen cloth.

8. Chop in a food processor or place in a mortar and pound with a pestle until smooth. Stir in the sugar and salt.

9. Dip a tree-shaped cookie cutter in water. Place on a clean dry cutting board and fill with rice. Press down with your fingers to compact the rice.

10. Spoon some pea mixture on top and carefully remove the cutter. Repeat with a quarter of the rice.

11. Pink Heart Sushi: Lay the smoked salmon (or ham) out on a clean dry cutting board. Use a heart-shaped cookie cutter to cut out shapes.

12. Dip the cutter in water. Place the cutter on a clean dry cutting board and fill with rice. Press down with your fingers to compact the rice.

13. Place a heart-shaped piece of salmon on top. Carefully remove the cutter. Repeat with a quarter of the rice.

14. White Knight Sushi: Peel the cucumber and slice thinly. Use a plain round cookie cutter to cut out slices.

15. Dip the cutter in water. Place on a clean dry cutting board and fill with rice. Press down with your fingers to compact the rice.

16. Place a round of cucumber on top. Carefully remove the cutter.

17. Sprinkle with sesame seeds and decorate with microcress. Repeat with the remaining rice.

18. Arrange the sushi on a large platter or on single serving plates, and serve.

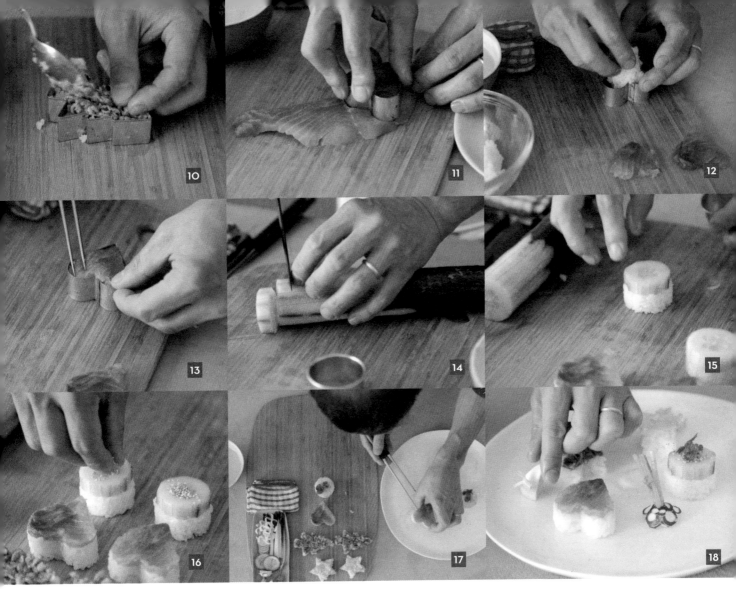

Children's Fruit Sushi

1	cup (200 g) sticky white rice
1¼	cups (310 ml) water
¼	cup (50 g) sugar
¼	cup (60 ml) coconut milk
¼	teaspoon salt
5–6	strawberries, thinly sliced
2–3	mandarins, peeled and divided into sections
2	kiwi fruit, peeled and thinly sliced
	Wedges of fresh or canned pineapple
	Other fruit, as desired
¾	cup (180 ml) vanilla yogurt, for dipping

• Combine the rice and water in a medium saucepan. Cover the pan, bring to a boil, and simmer until the water is almost all absorbed, about 15 minutes.

• Set aside for 15 minutes.

• Transfer the rice to a bowl. Stir in the sugar, then the coconut milk and salt. Set aside for 15 minutes.

• Dip your hands in cold water. Take about 1 tablespoon of rice and shape into an oval using your hands.

• Place on a baking sheet lined with parchment paper. Top with pieces of fruit. Press it lightly into the rice.

• Chill until ready to serve.

• Serve with the yogurt for dipping.

Sashimi

SASHIMI is a great delicacy and consists of very fresh fish thinly sliced and served raw.

1:41

SASHIMI is not sushi. Sushi is based on vinegared rice, whereas sashimi is very high quality fresh fish, which is served raw. We have included some recipes here because sashimi goes so very well with sushi and you may want to prepare a Japanese spread, including more than just sushi.

SASHIMI PLATTER

8	ounces (250 g) sashimi-grade fresh mackerel fillets, with skin
½	cup (100 g) coarse sea salt
½	cup (120 ml) rice vinegar
2	tablespoons water
½	tablespoon sugar
½	tablespoon mirin
8	ounces (250 g) sashimi-grade fresh sea bream fillets, skin and bones removed
2–3	paper-thin slices unwaxed lemon
8	ounces (250 g) sashimi-grade fresh tuna, skin and bones removed
8	ounces (250 g) sashimi-grade fresh salmon, skin and bones removed
	Shredded daikon, shiso (perilla) leaves, Wasabi paste, soy sauce, to garnish and serve

OPPOSITE: SASHIMI PLATTER

Sashimi Platter
Step by step

1. Mackerel: Lay the mackerel fillets in a large shallow bowl and sprinkle with the salt. Carefully rub the fillets with the salt.

2. Transfer to a colander and let drain for 3–4 hours.

3. Rinse carefully to remove excess salt and dry with a clean kitchen towel.

4. Mix the rice vinegar, water, sugar, and mirin in a small bowl or pitcher (jug),

stirring until the sugar is dissolved.

5. Place the mackerel in a shallow dish and pour the vinegar mixture over the top. Let marinate for 1 hour. The flesh will whiten.

6. Remove the fillets from the marinade and carefully remove the thin outer skin. Leave the iridescent underskin on the fish. Set aside on a platter.

7. Tuna: Place the tuna on a clean dry

VARIATION   SERVES **4–6**   PREPARATION **15 MINUTES**   COOKING **10–15 MINUTES**

Red Snapper Sashimi

Mustard & Miso Sauce
2   large egg yolks
¾   cup (200 g) white miso
2   tablespoons saké
2   tablespoons dark brown sugar
½   cup (120 ml) + 2 tablespoons water
3   tablespoons powder mustard
3   tablespoons rice vinegar

Sashimi
1   pound (500 g) sashimi-grade fresh red snapper fillets, skin and bones removed
3   cloves garlic, minced
1   (2-inch/5-cm) piece fresh ginger, peeled and finely grated
2   tablespoons white sesame seeds, toasted
12   fresh chives

• Whisk the egg yolks, miso, saké, and brown sugar in a small bowl.

• Whisk in ½ cup (120 ml) of water.

• Place in a double boiler over barely simmering water and stir until thickened.

• Remove from the heat and let cool to room temperature. Chill until needed.

• Cut the snapper into thin slices.

• Arrange the slices on serving plates. Dab with garlic and ginger. Sprinkle with the sesame seeds and chives.

• Blend the mustard powder with the remaining 2 tablespoons of water. Stir into the sauce along with the rice vinegar.

• Drizzle each portion with sauce, and serve.

7. chopping board and slice into pieces about ¼ inch (5 mm). Set aside.

8. Salmon: Place the salmon on a clean dry chopping board and slice into pieces about ¼ inch (5 mm). Set aside.

9. Sea Bream: Lay the fillets on a clean dry chopping board and slice thinly on an angle. Set aside.

10. Mackerel: Place on a clean dry cutting board and thinly slice across the fillets.

11. Garnish serving dishes with daikon. Use tongs to arrange slices of the fish on top.

12. Garnish the serving dishes to your liking with shiso leaves, carrot, lemon, and wasabi, and serve.

VARIATION   SERVES **4–6**   PREPARATION **20 MINUTES + 24 HOURS TO MARINATE**   COOKING **5 MINUTES**

Yellowtail & Lemon Sashimi

Tosa Soy Sauce
2	tablespoons mirin
5	teaspoons of saké
1	(2-inch/5-cm) square dried kombu, wiped
1	cup (250 ml) dark soy sauce
	Handfuls of dried bonito flakes

Sashimi
1	pound (500 g) sashimi-quality yellowtail fillets, skin and bones removed
2	unwaxed lemons
4	scallions (green onions), pale green and white parts only, thinly sliced
	Carrot curls, to garnish

• Heat the mirin and saké in a small pan until it produces fumes. Light with a long-handled match to burn off the alcohol.

• Combine kombu, soy sauce, and bonito flakes in a bowl and let marinate in the refrigerator for 24 hours.

• Strain the liquid into a jar, cover, and store in a dark cool place. It is best if kept for 1 month before serving.

• Slice the yellowtail into thin slices.

• Cut the lemons in half and remove the seeds. Slice into paper-thin slices.

• Arrange slices of lemon around the edges of each serving plate. Cover with slices of yellowtail that have been carefully rolled to fit.

• Pile with the scallions and carrot curls in the center of the plates.

• Serve with the tosa soy sauce.

Sashimi Salads

TRADITIONALLY, sashimi is served by itself but you can also serve it with fresh salad greens.

2:39

COMPLETE your sushi spread with one of our tasty salads. Sushi goes very well with fresh fish and the salads in this chapter will enable you to serve a light and healthy accompaniment to the sushi you have prepared.

SEARED TUNA SASHIMI SALAD

Tuna

8	ounces (250 g) sashimi-grade fresh bluefin tuna fillet, in 1 piece
	Salt and freshly ground black pepper
1	tablespoon grapeseed oil

Salad

1	cucumber
2	baby daikon
½	endive (chicory)
½	red endive (treviso)
1	celery stalk
2	radishes
1	asparagus spear
1	carrot
2	myoga ginger (ginger bud)
2	ounces (60 g) lotus root
	Watercress, to garnish

Dressing

1	small white onion, minced
4	tablespoons soy sauce
2	tablespoons rice vinegar
1	teaspoon sugar
½	teaspoon Japanese-style mustard powder
1	tablespoon water
2	tablespoons grapeseed oil
2	tablespoons sesame oil

OPPOSITE: SEARED TUNA SASHIMI SALAD

Seared Tuna Sashimi Salad
Step by step

1. Tuna: Season the tuna with salt and pepper.
2. Heat the oil in a grill pan (griddle) over high heat.
3. Sear all six sides of the tuna.
4. When seared all over, plunge the tuna into a bowl of iced water.
5. Remove and pat dry with paper towels.
6. Salad: Shave all the vegetables very thinly using a vegetable peeler into a bowl of iced water. Leave for 5 minutes.
7. Dressing: Rinse the onion in cold water to lessen its sharp flavor. Drain well.
8. Whisk the onion, soy sauce, vinegar, sugar, mustard powder, water, salt, and black pepper in a bowl.
9. When the salt has dissolved, add the grapeseed and sesame oils, blending well.
10. Drain the vegetables, tossing well to dry. Make heaps of vegetables in the center of the serving plates.
11. Cut the tuna fillet into slices about ⅛ inch (3 mm) thick.
12. Roll the slices into cylinders.
13. Arrange the tuna rolls around the vegetables on the plates.
14. Spoon the dressing over the tuna rolls and salads on the plates.
15. Garnish with the watercress, and serve.

VARIATION SERVES **4–6** PREPARATION **30 MINUTES** + TIME FOR THE RICE COOKING **2 MINUTES**

Seared Squid with Sushi Rice Salad

	Handful of fresh mint, parsley, and cilantro (coriander)
1	(2-inch/5-cm) piece ginger, minced
1	clove garlic, minced
1	lime, juice only
1	tablespoon light soy sauce
1	tablespoon honey
4	tablespoons (60 ml) sunflower oil
2	tablespoons sweet chili sauce
2	large squid, cleaned and sliced
	Salt and freshly ground black pepper
1	small cucumber, thinly diced
4	scallions (spring onions), thinly sliced
1	red chili, seeded and very thinly sliced
2	tablespoons pickled ginger, chopped
1	recipe sushi rice (see pages 14–17)

• Combine the herbs, ginger, lime juice, soy sauce, honey, and 3 tablespoons of oil in a food processor and chop until smooth. Chill until needed.

• Heat a grill pan or wok over high heat.

• Mix the chili sauce and remaining oil and brush over the squid.

• Season with salt and pepper.

• Sear the squid for 1 minute on each side.

• Toss all the salad ingredients in a bowl.

• To serve, divide the rice evenly among four to six plates and top each with some salad and squid. Finish with a drizzle of the dressing, and serve.

VARIATION SERVES **6–8** PREPARATION **30 MINUTES** + TIME FOR THE RICE **& 1 HOUR TO MARINATE** COOKING **5–10 MINUTES**

Seared Salmon with Sushi Rice Salad

1	pound (500 g) salmon fillets, skinned
1	(2-inch/5-cm) piece ginger, minced
2	cloves garlic, finely chopped
1	scallion (spring onion), finely chopped
1	tablespoon coriander seeds, crushed
	Salt and freshly ground black pepper
4	tablespoons (60 ml) saké
1	small pineapple, peeled and diced
1	tablespoon butter
1	tablespoon red pepper flakes
1	avocado, peeled, pitted, and diced
1	small cucumber, diced
1	large tomato, diced
1	bunch cilantro (coriander), chopped
1	recipe sushi rice (see pages 14–17)

• Combine the salmon, ginger, garlic, scallion, coriander, salt, and pepper in a bowl. Drizzle with the saké and let stand for 1 hour.

• Melt the butter in a medium pan until bubbling. Add the red pepper flakes, pineapple, and 2 tablespoons of the saké marinade. Cook down until all the liquid has evaporated.

• Heat a wok over high heat.

• Sear the salmon in the pan for 1–2 minutes. Remove from the pan and reserve

• Stir the avocado, cucumber, tomato, and cilantro into the rice.

• Divide evenly among six to eight serving plates.

• Slice the salmon and place on top of the rice.

• Spoon the pineapple mixture over the top, and serve immediately.

Miso Soups

MISO SOUPS are very popular in Japanese cuisine. In sushi bars a bowl of steaming miso soup is often served to finish the meal.

1:44

MISO is a type of fermented bean paste. With its delicious aroma and taste, miso is a staple ingredient in Japanese cooking and is used in a variety of dishes, from dressings for vegetables and grilled foods to pickling; but it is most commonly used to flavor miso soups. There are several kinds of miso, although they

are all made in the same way, by crushing boiled soybeans and adding wheat, barley, or rice, and injecting the mixture with a yeastlike mold. The mixture is left to mature for several months. You can buy miso pastes in jars or tubes from Japanese food stores. It keeps well in the refrigerator.

FENNEL MISO

2	tablespoons sesame oil
1	pound (500 g) fennel bulbs, finely sliced
1	carrot, julienned
	Whites of 2 leeks, sliced
2	potatoes, peeled and diced
1	(1-inch/2.5-cm) piece fresh ginger, peeled and finely chopped
1	clove garlic, finely chopped
½	small green chili, sliced
1	small red chili, sliced
1	teaspoon fennel seeds
	Salt
3	tablespoons red barley miso paste
6	cups (1.5 liters) boiling dashi stock (see page 76) or water
3	cups (150 g) watercress, chopped + extra, to garnish
5	snow peas (mangetout), halved
1	tablespoon freshly squeezed lemon juice

OPPOSITE: FENNEL MISO

Fennel Miso
Step by step

1. Heat the oil in a large soup pot over medium heat.
2. Add the fennel, carrot, leeks, and potatoes and sauté until the vegetables are softened, 4–5 minutes.
3. Stir in the ginger, garlic, chilies, and fennel seeds. Season with salt and sauté over low heat for 10 minutes.
4. Dissolve the miso in ½ cup (120 ml) of the boiling dashi stock or water.
5. Stir the miso mixture and remaining dashi stock or water into the soup.
6. Simmer until the potatoes are tender, 15–20 minutes.
7. Add the watercress, snow peas, and lemon juice. Simmer for 3 minutes more.
8. Squeeze the lemon juice into the soup.
9. Ladle into serving bowls.
10. Garnish with the extra watercress and serve hot.

Shrimp & Udon Noodle Miso

12	ounces (350 g) dried udon noodles
24	(about 1 pound/500 g) small cooked shrimp (prawns), peeled, heads removed
5	ounces (150 g) silken firm tofu, cut into small squares
8	cups (2 liters) water
¾	cup (200 g) white miso paste
1	tablespoon finely grated fresh ginger
2	tablespoons soy sauce
1	bunch asparagus, trimmed, cut into lengths on the diagonal
12	ounces (350 g) mixed Asian mushrooms (oyster, shimeji, shiitake, etc)
2	cups (100 g) baby spinach leaves
2	scallions (spring onions), trimmed, thinly sliced on the diagonal

· Cook the noodles in a large saucepan of boiling water until just tender, about 8 minutes, or according to the instructions on the package. Drain well.

· Divide the noodles evenly among six to eight serving bowls.

· Top each bowl with some shrimp and tofu.

· Put the water and miso paste in a medium saucepan over medium-high heat. Bring to a boil, whisking often, until the miso dissolves.

· Reduce the heat to low. Add the ginger and soy sauce and simmer for 2 minutes.

· Add the asparagus, mushrooms, and spinach, and simmer for 30 seconds, until the spinach is just wilted.

· Ladle the soup into the bowls over the noodles.

· Sprinkle with the scallions, and serve hot.

Soba Noodle Miso

½	ounce (15 g) dried shiitake mushrooms
1½	cups (375 ml) boiling water
8	ounces (250 g) dried soba noodles
8	cups (2 liters) water
1	(1-inch/2.5-cm) piece fresh ginger, peeled and thinly sliced
2	tablespoons red barley miso paste
3	tablespoons white miso paste
3	scallions (spring onions), thinly sliced diagonally
4	ounces (120 g) button mushrooms, sliced

· Soak the shiitake mushrooms in the boiling water for 30 minutes.

· Drain, reserving the liquid. Thinly slice the mushrooms.

· Cook the noodles in a large pan of boiling water until tender, 4–5 minutes. Drain.

· Place the water, ginger, and reserved soaking liquid in a saucepan over high heat. Bring to a boil, then decrease the heat to low.

· Add both miso pastes and whisk until combined.

· Add the scallions, shiitake, and button mushrooms, and stir until well combined.

· Divide the noodles and soup evenly among serving bowls. Serve hot.

Salads

IF you are preparing a Japanese sushi meal for guests, you may also want to add a salad or two to the spread.

JAPANESE SALADS are often based on cool or chilled udon or soba noodles. These salads are especially popular in lunch boxes during the hot summer months, but they are also good to accompany sushi dishes. Serve with soy sauce for dipping. Sunomono, or cucumber salad, is another classic Japanese salad. It is easy to make, healthy to eat, and very refreshing when served with other dishes.

COOL NOODLE SALAD

Salad

8	ounces (250 g) udon noodles
8	ounces (250 g) snow peas (mangetout)
2	cos (romaine/little gem) lettuces, leaves separated
2	carrots
1	cucumber
4	medium vine tomatoes
	Sea salt flakes

Dressing

3	tablespoons Japanese soy sauce
2	tablespoons sugar
2	tablespoons rice vinegar
1½	tablespoons sesame oil
½	cup (120 ml) cold water

OPPOSITE: COOL NOODLE SALAD

Cool Noodle Salad
Step by step

1. Heat a large pot of water over high heat. Add a good pinch of salt.

2. Add the noodles to the boiling water and cook for the time indicated on the package.

3. Drain well, and rinse under cold running water. Drain again.

4. Place in a bowl of ice water.

5. Scoop the noodles our of the water in handfuls, squeezing them to remove as much moisture as possible.

6. Shape the squeezed handfuls of noodles into nests and set aside on a plate.

7. Blanch the snow peas in a pot of boiling water for 1–2 minutes.

8. Drain well, place in a bowl of ice water, then drain again. Dry in a clean kitchen cloth or with paper towels.

9. Wash the lettuces and dry well on paper towels.

10. Cut the carrots and cucumber into matchsticks and set aside.

11. Thinly slice the lettuce leaves and snow peas. Set aide.

12. Cut the tomatoes in thin wedges.

13. Combine all the dressing ingredients in a bowl and stir until the sugar has dissolved.

14. Divide the noodles and vegetables among six serving bowls.

15. Drizzle the dressing over the salads, and serve.

VARIATION SERVES **4–6** PREPARATION **10 MINUTES**

Cucumber Salad

3	Japanese or 4 Persian cucumbers
½	teaspoon salt
¼	cup (60 ml) rice vinegar
1½	tablespoons sugar
½	teaspoon soy sauce
1	tablespoon white sesame seeds

• Slice the cucumbers crosswise as thinly as possible.

• Place in a bowl with the salt and let rest for 5 minutes.

• Use your hands to squeeze the moisture out of the cucumbers.

• Whisk the rice vinegar, sugar, and soy sauce in a small bowl until the sugar dissolves.

• Add the vinegar mixture and sesame seeds to the cucumbers, mix well, and serve.

VARIATION SERVES **4–6** PREPARATION **15 MINUTES** COOKING **5–10 MINUTES**

Shrimp & Noodle Salad

Salad

¼	cup sesame seeds
7	ounces (200 g) udon noodles
1	pound (500 g) small shelled, cooked shrimp (prawns)
8	scallions (spring onions), thinly sliced
1	tablespoon shredded ao-nori (dried seaweed)

Dressing

1	tablespoon soy sauce
½	cup (120 ml) saké
2	tablespoons finely grated fresh ginger
2	cloves garlic, minced
1	tablespoon sesame oil

• Place the sesame seeds in a small dry frying pan. Cook, stirring, until lightly browned, 2–3 minutes. Set aside.

• Cook the noodles and dry them following the instructions in the video and step by step.

• Shape the squeezed handfuls of noodles into nests and set aside on a plate.

• Add the shrimp, scallions, and sesame seeds to the noodles and toss well.

Dressing

• Combine all the dressing ingredients in a small bowl and mix well.

• Drizzle the dressing over the salad.

• Top with the shredded seaweed, and serve.

Garnishes

PRESENTATION is key when serving sushi.

You want the food to look as good as it tastes.

1:24

GARNISHES

1   medium carrot

1   medium cucumber

1   lemon

GARNISHING the finished dishes is very much a matter of personal taste. As with most things Japanese, simplicity and elegance are the two main goals. Less is more to the Japanese eye, so don't overload each dish with garnishes. A paper-thin slice of lemon, a twirl of pickled ginger, or a wrap of thinly sliced cucumber are often enough. Here we have shown you how make a clever twist of carrot, a cucumber basket, and an elegant lemon wedge. With a sharp knife, some very fresh vegetables, and a little imagination you could also create many other garnishes.

OPPOSITE: PLATTER OF SIMPLE GARNISHES

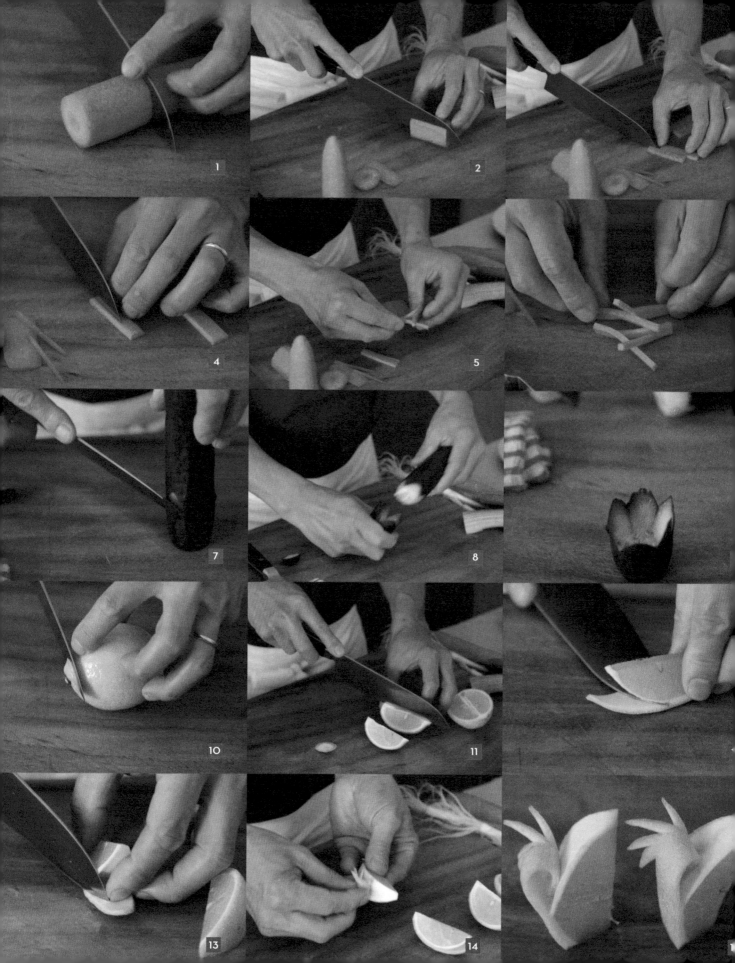

Garnishes
Step by step

Keep color in mind when choosing the garnishes for each dish. Decide if you want to contrast or blend with the food and the serving dish. Sushi is often served on simple wooden platters, or minimalist Japanese-style mono or duo-toned ceramic dishes. These work well with a burst of color from a carrot, or a cucumber or lemon.

1. Carrot Garnish: Scrape a medium carrot. Cut into three even lengths.

2. Slice the lengths about ¼ inch (5 mm) thick.

3. Trim off the rounded edges then cut the pieces in half lengthwise.

4. Cut each half piece one-third of the way in for about two-thirds of its length. Turn and slice on the other side in the same way.

5. Pull the cut pieces of carrot to form a kind of crossed A shape.

6. Make several more in the same way and use them to garnish dishes with sushi rolls.

7. Cucumber Garnish: Trim the end off a cucumber. Make six neat incisions all around the cucumber about 1 inch (2.5 cm) up from the work surface.

8. Twist off the piece of cucumber.

9. Place the resulting little basket-shaped piece of cucumber upright and use to garnish. Trim the end off the remaining cucumber and repeat to make as many garnishes as possible.

10. Lemon Garnish: Trim the end off a lemon.

11. Slice the lemon in half lengthwise and then in half again.

12. Using a sharp knife, cut the yellow and white peel away from the flesh about two-thirds of the way down.

13. Slice the peel thinly on the diagonal on one side.

14. Fold the peel under so that the sliced pieces stick up.

15. Repeat with the remaining quarters of lemon. Use as a garnish.

Pickles & Sauces

SUSHI is usually served with condiments, such as soy sauce or wasabi. But there are many others that you can buy or make at home.

2:23

THE MOST COMMON condiments for sushi are shōyu (Japanese soy sauce) and wasabi. The soy sauce is usually served in little bowls so that diners can dip their sushi in to flavor as they eat. Bright green and spicy, wasabi is often included inside the rolls, but extra wasabi is also usually included on the serving platter. Pickled ginger is another favorite accompaniment, although it was originally intended as a palate cleanser and served between courses. Here we have featured a delicious recipe for pickled vegetables which can be served with a range of dishes, from sushi rolls and cones to sashimi.

MIXED PICKLED VEGETABLES

1	small cucumber, about 6 inches (15 cm) long
1	medium carrot
1	daikon radish
6–8	red radishes, tops removed
¼	small green cabbage
6	cloves garlic, thinly sliced
2	teaspoons salt
½	lemon, juiced
1	cup (250 ml) rice vinegar
¾	cup (150 g) sugar
¼	cup (60 ml) water

OPPOSITE: MIXED PICKLED VEGETABLES

Mixed Pickled Vegetables
Step by step

1. Cut the cucumber in half lengthwise and use a teaspoon to scoop out the seeds.
2. Cut the halves lengthwise into three long strips. Slice crosswise into very thin strips.
3. Scrape the carrot then cut into three pieces crosswise. Slice each piece thinly, then cut into very thin strips.
4. Peel the daikon radish using a knife.
5. Trim off the top and bottom. Slice each piece thinly, then cut into very thin strips.
6. Slice the radishes into 3 or 4 pieces crosswise, then cut into very thin strips.
7. Slice the cabbage into ½-inch (1-cm) strips.
8. Put all the vegetables and the garlic into a bowl. Sprinkle with the salt.
9. Mix well with your hands to coat with the salt. Set aside for 30 minutes.
10. Rinse the vegetables under cold running water.
11. Drain well, squeezing out the excess moisture by hand. Place in a bowl. Drizzle with the lemon juice.
12. Combine the rice vinegar, sugar, and water in a saucepan over medium-high heat and bring to a boil, stirring until the sugar has dissolved. Simmer for 5 minutes.
13. Remove from the heat and pour into a small pitcher (jug) or bowl to cool.
14. Pour the vinegar mixture over the vegetables in the bowl.
15. Cover the bowl with plastic wrap (cling film) and chill for 24 hours, or until ready to serve.

VARIATION MAKES **1¼ CUPS (300 ML)** PREPARATION **5 MINUTES**

Spicy Mayonnaise

1	cup (250 ml) Japanese mayonnaise (or normal mayonnaise)
4	tablespoons (60 ml) Sriracha or other very spicy sweet chili sauce
1	teaspoon sesame oil

• Put the mayonnaise in a small ceramic or glass bowl. Gradually stir in the Sriracha sauce and sesame oil, mixing until blended and pale pink.

• Pour into a bowl or jar, cover, and chill until required.

• Use the sauce as directed in the recipes, or instead of wasabi. You can also serve it as a dipping sauce with other sushi dishes.

• Keeps 2–3 days in the refrigerator.

VARIATION MAKES **ABOUT 2 CUPS** PREPARATION **15 MINUTES + 2–3 HOURS TO REST & 5–7 DAYS TO PICKLE** COOKING **5 MINUTES**

Pickled Ginger

8	ounces (250 g) fresh young ginger root
2	teaspoons salt
1	cup (250 ml) rice vinegar
⅓	cup (90 ml) water
4	tablespoons sugar

• Wash the ginger carefully and scrub off the skin. Slice thinly with a sharp knife and place in a shallow bowl. Sprinkle with the salt and leave to rest for 2–3 hours.

• Dry the slices of ginger with paper towels and place in a sterilized glass jar.

• Mix the rice vinegar, water, and sugar in a small saucepan over medium heat, stirring until the sugar is dissolved. Bring to a boil then remove from the heat.

• Pour the hot vinegar mixture into the jar over the ginger. Let cool and leave to pickle in the marinade, 5–7 days. As the ginger pickles it will turn a pale pink color.

• Allow about 2 tablespoons for each person when serving.

• Keeps in the refrigerator for several weeks.

Index

A, B

Avocado Inside-Out Rolls 22
Avocado Sushi Balls 71
Bell Pepper Nigiri 59
Brown Sushi Rice 17

C

California Sushi Rolls 36
Carpaccio Nigiri in Chicory Boats 58
Children's Fruit Sushi 95
Children's Mixed Sushi 92
Cool Noodle Salad 108
Cucumber Rolls 20
Cucumber Salad 111

E, F

Easy Scattered Sushi 83
Fennel Miso 104
Fresh Salmon & Avocado Rolls with
    Salmon Roe 21
Fresh Salmon Pressed Sushi with Nori
    & Fish Roe 55
Fresh Tuna Rolls 29

G

Garnishes 112
Grilled Mackerel Bo Sushi 42

I, J

Inside-out Chicken & Cream Cheese
    Rolls with Dill 40
Inside-Out Grilled Salmon & Cream
    Cheese Rolls 41
Inside-Out Rolls with Scallops
    & Cilantro 25

Inside-Out Rolls with Smoked Salmon
    & Dill 25
Inside-Out Spicy Ham & Cream
    Cheese Rolls 40
Inside-Out Vegetarian Rolls 38
Japanese Omelet Nigiri 60

M

Mixed Fish Roe Warship Sushi 64
Mixed Pickled Vegetables 116
Mixed Seafood Cones 46
Mixed Seafood Nigiri Platter 56
Mixed Sushi Ball Platter 68
Moneybag Sushi 88
Mushroom Inari 87

P, Q

Philadelphia Rolls 39
Pickled Ginger 119
Pressed Sushi with Marinated
    Mackerel 50
Quinoa Inari 87

R, S

Red Snapper Sashimi 98
Roasted Vegetable Rolls 29
Salmon, Crab & Avocado Rolls 26
Sashimi Platter 96
Scattered Sushi, Edo Style 76
Scattered Sushi, Kansi Style 80
Seared Beef Rolls 32
Seared Salmon with Sushi Rice Salad
    103
Seared Squid with Sushi Rice Salad
    103

Seared Tuna Sashimi Salad 100
Shrimp & Avocado Rolls 31
Shrimp & Noodle Salad 111
Shrimp & Udon Noodle Miso 107
Shrimp Salad Warships 67
Shrimp Sushi Cones 49
Smoked Chicken & Apple Pressed
    Sushi 54
Smoked Salmon & Lime Pressed Sushi
    54
Smoked Salmon Sushi Wraps 35
Soba Noodle Miso 107
Spicy Mayonnaise 119
Spicy Shrimp Inari 84
Spring Festival Scattered Sushi 83
Stuffed Squid Sushi 72
Sushi Rice 14

T

Teriyaki Beef Rolls 30
Teriyaki Chicken Warships 67
Tuna & Cucumber Rolls 30
Tuna & Salmon Scattered Sushi 79
Tuna & Wasabi Rolls 18

V, Y

Vegetarian Sushi Balls 70
Vegetarian Sushi Cones 48
Yellowtail & Flying Fish Roe Pressed
    Sushi 53
Yellowtail & Lemon Sashimi 99